READERS' FAVORITE™ FIVE-STAR AWARD WINNER

"...I really enjoyed reading this book...

It helped me understand my dad and our relationship even more. I highly recommend it for all fathers and daughters... Your relation ship will never be the same."

   – Joy Hannabass for Readers' Favorite™

= =

"Surprisingly candid... terrifically rewarding"

"For women, here's **an emotional glimpse into the complex relationship between fathers and their daughters** – from a father's perspective. Being the father of a daughter myself, I was really moved by the joys and heartaches many of these dads were willing to share."

   – Steve Harrison, Publisher
      Radio-TV Interview Report (RTIR)

You think you know your father.

But what if you missed something so subtle and yet so profound that it will change your understanding of what MEN are really like?

THE SECRET LIFE
OF **FATHERS**

From Intimate Interviews With
101 Fathers of Daughters

2ND **EDITION**
UPDATED WITH NEW SECTIONS ADDED

Edited by James I. Bond
Founder of **THE FATHER-DAUGHTER PROJECT**™

Contact: jbond@TheFatherDaughterProject.com

www.TheFatherDaughterProject.com

Publisher's Cataloging-In-Publication Data
(Prepared by The Donohue Group, Inc.)

Names: Bond, James I., editor.
Title: The secret life of fathers : from intimate interviews with 101 fathers of daughters / edited by
    James I. Bond, founder of The Father-Daughter Project.
Description: Second edition, updated with new sections added. | Thousand Oaks, California : U.S.
    Management, LLC, Publishing Div., [2017] | Previously published: North Charleston, South
    Carolina : CreateSpace Independent Publishing Platform, 2013.
ISBN-10: 0998865702
Identifiers: ISBN 9780998865706 | ISBN 978-0-9988657-1-3 (ebook)
Subjects: LCSH: Fathers and daughters--Anecdotes. | Fathers--Interviews. | Fatherhood--
    Anecdotes. | Man-woman relationships--Anecdotes. | Mothers and sons--Anecdotes. | LCGFT:
    Anecdotes. | Interviews.
Classification: LCC HQ755.85 .S43 2017 (print) | LCC HQ755.85 (ebook) | DDC
    306.874/2--dc23

This book is dedicated with

the deepest love and affection

to my daughters Morgan, Lauren

and Erin.

The complexity of my relationships

with each of you has

profoundly troubled and fulfilled me,

in ways that perhaps only a father of daughters

could truly understand.

Learn more about the fathers in this book by visiting our website at

www.TheFatherDaughterProject.com

Also, visit us to share your own father-daughter story

By sharing your own personal story, you may inspire
a father or a daughter in ways that you may not even realize.

In this way, we may all contribute to helping
create a world that is more caring and compassionate.

CONTENTS

ACKNOWLEDGEMENTS

"It takes a village"

A book like this could not be created without the loving support and assistance of many people.

First and foremost, I thank my wife Pam for putting up with more than seven years of preparation, research, struggles, requests for feedback, and more. Your encouragement and insights through all this made my dream and journey to make a difference possible.

I thank all the fathers who so graciously agreed to be interviewed, that your stories and insights may help other fathers and daughters to understand and strengthen their own father-daughter relationships.

I thank my three daughters, Morgan, Lauren and Erin. Your inspiration, perspective and feedback throughout the process helped sharpen the relevance of the material for me, and hopefully for others who read these pages. I also hope my connections with you have been enriched from my having gone through this experience.

I thank my faithful and diligent assistant Adam Tan. Your hard work and care from the first recordings through to the book's completion, creation of the website and more, have helped me bring this work to life.

I thank my brother-in-law Rick Elger for coming up with a title that resonates for me, and hopefully for others—The Secret Life of Fathers. Your willingness to review the manuscript and your creativity and unique perspective have helped raise the bar for a book I have worked so hard to make relevant and resonant.

I thank Steve Harrison, publicity and marketing coach extraordinaire, for your support and guidance, in helping me create a book I am proud of. You empowered me go back to the drawing board and let the book evolve naturally, encouraging me to trust that my instincts would guide me to create something important, something that could have a positive impact on fathers and daughters who read it.

I thank the Mankind Project for helping me gain a perspective on the unexpressed feelings of so many fathers, and later, for helping me find many of the fathers of daughters who were willing to share their stories and insights.

I thank my mom for so graciously sharing your personal father-daughter stories with me. You helped me understand that mothers are also daughters, holding powerful, sometimes painful connections with the past... with fathers who may not have been aware of their profound impact on his impressionable little girl. Through your discussions and stories, I began to realize how the early impact of a father could plant seeds that last a lifetime.

I thank my dad for graciously agreeing to be the first father interviewed. Your support and particularly your impatience helped me mold the subsequent interviews into meaningful, emotional exposes where even the most impatient and reserved dads felt safe and comfortable sharing many of their most personal stories and insights.

I thank my brother Howard. Your early assistance and camaraderie helped open the door to this powerful work, enabling me to transform it from a simple question by a struggling father trying to improve my relationship with my daughters, into a project that could impact others.

I thank all the clients, the professionals, the PhDs and other specialists in psychology and organizational development involved with Leadership Management Associates of California, Inc., the training and behavior management company I ran for more than 12 years. You helped me transform a simple training company into a laboratory of human behavior that opened the eyes, hearts and minds of so many who were touched by the powerful work we did... while laying the foundation for what has become The Father-Daughter project.

I thank my brother John and sister Baila for your support and advice through the months and years of this process. Your input helped me maintain this as a work of love and not convert it into an academic project.

I thank my writer's group, Deb, Katie, and all the others, who continually pushed me to create writing that resonates in ways I never before believed I could.

I thank Deb Englander, who provided such valuable input into improving the structure of the book. I believe your pushing me to add my personal comments throughout has made it accessible and relevant to more people.

I thank all the family, friends and strangers who read through the numerous manuscripts and excerpts, providing advice and insight that contributed so much to the book and to the work we're doing with The Father-Daughter Project.

And lastly, I thank you for reading this book. Hopefully our work with The Father-Daughter Project will help to further enhance your life in some large or small way.

We at The Father-Daughter Project are grateful to all of you, and humbled that you have allowed us to share this work with you. May your future be a wondrous canvas for the life you've always wanted to live.

THE SECRET LIFE
OF **FATHERS**

Paul McCartney's Daughter Talks About Her Dad

 I distinctly remember when we were kids, and he'd play his guitar and we would say, **'Dad, can you shut up, we are trying to watch television.'** And he would then say: **'Do you kids know how many people out there actually appreciate my playing?'**

Naturally, he's not Sir Paul McCartney to me, but just my dad who makes me laugh and smile."

- Mary McCartney

(Source: Star-Telegram, May 13, 2007)

A Message to Girls and Women

Could a lifetime of bad decisions be the result of your father ...not having eye contact with you at the dinner table?

Remember, your father was the first man in your life.

Whether you realize it or not, he's had a profound influence on you.

But what if you missed something?

What if, deep down, there's something about your dad that you didn't realize... something that could change your understanding of what men are really like?

Readers of this Book Speak Out

Did I Misunderstand Who My Father REALLY Was...

 [Reading this book] I learned things I would never have guessed about men. I felt recognized by some of their insights about what a daughter needs (a safe place, guidance, encouragement, love).

I didn't get much of that from my dad.

After reading the interviews in this book, I wonder if my dad wanted to be more involved, but didn't know how.

I think this should be required reading for all dads of daughters, so they don't end up regretting what they missed, and so their daughters can look back later and say, "You were a loving, supportive dad!"

And daughters should read it too, so they know what makes their dad tick."

- Maggie Dennison,
Marketing Coach and Writer

Deep Down, Was My Father SCARED of His Daughters...

 This was a very interesting and sweet look into the minds of fathers who have daughters.

I never realized why my father did some of the things he did, and I probably criticized him more than I should have sometimes, having the perception that he didn't care, when he was really just scared and uncertain about how to deal with my sisters and me.

The revelation I got from reading this book has improved my relationship with my father, and I know it will help me be a better wife and mother in the future."

- Lauren Aja Bond
(the author's daughter)

Why Men Hide Their Most Important Emotions

Here's the Reason It May Be Difficult to Understand What Your Father is Really Like

To understand why father-daughter relationships can be complicated, it may help to understand something that happens to a man when he's inside his mother's womb.

When I explained this to the host of a radio show, she started laughing on air and shouted out, "That explains a lot. I always knew men were brain-damaged!"

Hahaha...
I always knew
men were
brain-damaged!

So, what exactly are we talking about?

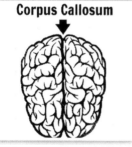

Corpus Callosum

At one point while in the womb, the male fetus gets a rush of testosterone. This eats away at the Corpus Callosum, which is the tissue that connects the right side of the brain (emotion) and the left side of the brain (speech, getting things done). [1] [2]

This may explain why men are generally able to turn off emotions more easily than women.[3] [4] [5] For early man, this may have enabled him to survive dangerous tasks such as hunting wild beasts, without getting overwhelmed by emotion.

Unfortunately, it may also explain why today, especially in relationships, so few men are comfortable exposing emotions that exhibit their "vulnerability."[6] [7] [8]

Anger and Silence...
These Often Mask A Man's True Feelings

So instead of showing fear, shame or hurt feelings, many men will disguise their emotions, through anger and aggression... or through silence... making it easy for people to misunderstand what they're REALLY feeling.

For this reason, you may find the quotes and excerpts in this book especially eye-opening. These highly personal comments from more than 100 fathers of daughters, often expose feelings and emotions that are rarely shared anywhere else.

Through these often-surprising comments, you may discover the father you thought you knew, may be somewhat different from what you expected.

References

1. Sex-related differences in the development of the human fetal corpus callosum: in utero ultrasonographic study, by R. Achiron, S. Lipitz, A. Achiron, (Diagnostic Ultrasound Unit, Department of Obstetrics and Gynecology, The Chaim Sheba Medical Center, Tel Hashomer, and Faculty of Medicine, Tel Aviv University, Israel), PubMed / National Institutes of Health, Feb. 21, 2001 (https://www.ncbi.nlm.nih.gov/pubmed/11241538)

2. Handbook of Clinical Gender Medicine, Pg. 42 (Fetal Programming – The Sexual Dimorphous Brain; Organizational and Activational Effects of Sex Hormones), by Karin Schenck-Gustafsson and Paula R. DeCola, Karger Medical and Scientific Publishers. Aug. 17, 2012

3. Brain Differences Between Genders, by Gregory L. Jantz, PhD, Psychology Today, Feb. 27, 2014 (https://www.psychologytoday.com/blog/hope-relationships/201402/brain-differences-between-genders).

4. Fetal Testosterone May Program Boys' Behavior (excerpted from the journal Biological Psychiatry), Live Science (www.livescience.com/24540-fetal-testosterone-boys-impulsivity.html), Nov. 5, 2012

5. Prenatal testosterone and gender-related behavior, PubMed – National Institutes of Health (www.ncbi.nlm.nih.gov/pubmed/17074984), Nov 2006.

6. Fetal Testosterone Predicts Sexually Differentiated Childhood Behavior in Girls and in Boys, National Institutes of Health (www.ncbi.nlm.nih.gov/pmc/articles/PMC2778233), Nov 17, 2009

7. Prenatal testosterone influences adult men's behavior toward women, PsyPost, May 21, 2016

8. The hardwired difference between male and female brains could explain why men are better at map reading. (2013, December 3). Retrieved January 30, 2014, from www.independent.co.uk/life-style/the-hardwired-difference-between-male-and-female-brains-could-explain-why-men-are-better-at-map-reading-8978248.html.

What Is It About Women...
That Confuses Men and Dads?

I was once told, there are two ways a man screws up a relationship with a woman.

He talks... or he doesn't talk.

Funny as this comment might seem, there is a deeper truth here. Men are often fearful of opening their mouths in front of a woman, out of concern that their words will be taken the wrong way, or will trigger an unexpected emotional response. For a guy, sometimes listening may be safer than talking.

This is a legitimate concern, derived from the subtle and dramatic differences between men and women.

For example, are women (and daughters) more emotional than men?

If yes, is this a weakness or a strength?

The answers to these questions are not as simple as they may seem. And herein lies the reason so many men find their relationships with their daughters (and with women) to be complicated.

The 9-11 fireman we interviewed, said it best.

"I grew up in a household with two brothers, so to me, girls were aliens!"

Once he had a daughter, what he discovered was, in some ways women are wired differently than men. Not better or worse, just different.

Unfortunately, these differences can be disorienting and confusing for many men.

But there's hope!

Giving men (and fathers) an opportunity to better understand women, could go a long way to simplifying father-daughter and man-woman relationships.

So let's give it a try.

Did You Ever See A Woman Cry...

Before we discuss the differences between men and women, let's be clear that no two women and no two men are the same.

Still, there are traits that tend to be common among many men and women.

Let's start with emotions.

Studies have shown that women tend to feel negative emotions such as guilt, shame, and embarrassment more easily and more intensely than men often will. They may also feel an overwhelming sense of anxiety from a stressful situation more readily than a man might.[1]

Men get blindsided when they are not expecting such strong reactions, especially from what they may consider to be benign circumstances. ("I didn't think it was such a big deal, so I was surprised at how emotional she got over it.")

The relationship between a man and a woman can get even more complicated when she starts discussing a problem she's facing. That's because women will often be more interested in being heard than in having someone solve their problem.

For men who are natural problem-solvers, this can be confusing and frustrating.

But a man who learns to listen without always trying to solve a woman's problem, can greatly simplify and improve his relationships with his daughter, and with women.[2]

Can A Woman Read Your Mind...

The flip side of this may provide women with a powerful edge over men, in certain situations.

Although this won't apply to all women, in general, women can be more sensitive than men, to the emotions and feelings of others.[1] In professional situations that rely on recognizing the emotional states of others, like sales and therapy, women can be especially astute.

However, especially in father-daughter relations, it can be unnerving for a man to realize his daughter is always watching and evaluating him.

Dads who are willing to embrace a daughter's emotional sensitivity can benefit greatly. They can experience better empathy and self-awareness, while learning how to become more authentic (more comfortable being themselves), especially with women.

The downside of emotional sensitivity is that women can feel overwhelmed when they are rejected.[1] This creates a vulnerability that can be exploited by a manipulative man or woman, who is willing to feed and prey on a woman's self-esteem for their own personal gain.

With women so vulnerable to rejection, dads who ignore or somehow *reject* their daughters — accidentally or on purpose — can create emotional scars that will persist, perhaps throughout their entire lives.

The good news is, these scars can be healed if a dad is ultimately willing to rebuild or otherwise repair a connection with his daughter, even later in life.

By contrast, many men will resist any request for more intimacy in a relationship, and this could be a source of frustration in some women.[1]

Daddy Doesn't Love Me...
But I'm Afraid To Ask Him Why

On another front, women are more likely than men, to avoid risky situations.[3]

In some ways this can be good. But in others, it may periodically deprive her of easy solutions to relatively simple problems.

A perfect example is the woman who asked us at The Father-Daughter Project™ to interview her dad, in the hopes that he would reveal to us the reason he had abandoned her for more than a decade. (This is the last interview in this book).

For more than nine years, since she was 15 years old, this young lady had lived with seething guilt that she had somehow said or done something wrong, that caused her dad to cut off ties to her, and even change his phone number.

Deep down, she lived in fear and humiliation that she had somehow repelled her dad. What's worse, it made her afraid that she would somehow repel other men without knowing why. This had her living with an intense insecurity, especially when it came to dating men.

Finally, three years before our interview, she bumped into her dad in New York, and gleefully reunited with him. They were now enjoying a terrifically positive relationship... and she didn't want to say anything that might ruin it.

So she avoided the question of why he had abandoned her, a subject that deeply troubled her.

Had she been willing to take a chance and simply ask, she might have avoided years of life-changing feelings that all-but-killed her self-confidence, affecting just about every aspect of her life.

We've seen this often... a woman experiencing years or even decades of emotional pain because she was unwilling to ask a tough question for fear that it may jeopardize the harmony of a seemingly positive relationship.

Does this mean women are so risk-averse that they may actually hurt themselves as a result?

Fear Is A Funny Thing...

A landmark lawsuit by the Equal Employment Opportunity Commission (EEOC) against Sears department stores, supports this assertion.

In an effort to boost their own income, Sears gave all their floor sales-people the option to convert their pay to commission-only. To make it attractive, they ensured that everyone who switched would suddenly be earning more money.

The problem? Just about every man converted to the higher commission-only pay, but almost no women did. So suddenly, men were earning more than women.

The EEOC argued that to women, the "commission-only" structure felt more risky, so they resisted, and that was unfair.

The courts ultimately ruled that Sears could not be held responsible for a quirk in the human behavior of women.[4]

For many, this unusual case helped define women as risk-avoiders compared to men.

But even if it's true, is it such a terrible thing?

The insurance industry understands that men are better at getting themselves out of trouble when faced with a dangerous driving situation... but women are less likely to get themselves into a dangerous situation in the first place.[5]

And yes, it's true that many of the greatest advancements in science and business are the result of men taking hair-brained risks. But it's also true that men are just as responsible for many of the largest flame-outs in history.

Somehow, it seems the best traits in business and in life, lie somewhere between the toughness of men and the sensitivities of women.

The Fallacy That Women Are Bad Negotiators

Many of the dads we interviewed voiced a frustration that their daughters would take punishment and reward without debate or negotiation, whereas boys would tend to negotiate and bargain a little more often.

So, by nature, are women worse negotiators than men?

After all, to be an effective negotiator, you must be willing to face conflict and "rejection" by asking for more than the other person may be willing to give, without showing your emotional cards. In effect, you must be willing to walk away from the deal, or at least bluff, if you don't get what you want.

Could a woman do that?

One study of graduating MBA students found that half of men, but only about one-eighth of women actually negotiate when offered a job.[6]

In another example, tech giant Hewlett Packard wondered why so few women were applying for senior management positions within their company.

Their research uncovered a surprising fact. Women tended to apply only when they were 100% qualified for a position, while men only needed to be 60% qualified to feel they could apply.

From this study, a universal belief evolved that compared to men, women tend to work harder, but they also seem less confident of themselves.

However there is another possible explanation.

In a Harvard Business Review article, women's expert Tara Mohr explained how she believes women simply don't know the 'rules of the game.' Her premise is that women don't understand that it's okay to apply for a job, even if you're not fully qualified.

She believes women need to be taught that people with lesser qualifications often get these incredible jobs, simply because they applied.[7]

But who's going to teach women the 'rules of the game?'

Teach Me How To Play The Game... And Watch What Happens

Silicon Valley exec Ellen Pau believes the negotiation process is rigged against women. As she explained it to the Wall Street Journal, "Men negotiate harder than women do, and sometimes women get penalized when they do negotiate."[8]

In other words, women are criticized when they negotiate hard, so they resist. But it's changing.

When Sheryl Sandberg was offered the job of running Facebook, she was ready to accept CEO Mark Zuckerberg's first offer when her husband abruptly stopped her. Even though this was her dream job at an incredible pay, her husband explained that accepting the first offer 'is not the way the game is played!'

He got her to make a counter-offer, from which Zuckerberg came back with a much more lucrative proposal. Suddenly, she had learned a powerful lesson about the games played in a 'man's world.'

Sandberg often tells women's audiences that they need to learn how to play a game that's unfamiliar to many women.[9]

No Crying Please

So, are women doomed to be terrible negotiators, compared to men?

Absolutely not!

First, because of their emotional sensitivity, women can be more collaborative and more intuitive at reading the emotional state of their opponents better than men, giving them an edge.

Also, for whose women who are bold enough and confident enough, they can invent their own rules. They can dig into their own psychological tool box and thus, can totally disorient the men they are interacting with.

After all, have you ever seen a woman cry in the middle of an argument? Is she being emotionally overwhelmed or simply manipulative? (Hint: It may sometimes be a bit of both).

Of course, crying may not always be an option.

Movie producer Laura Ziskin told me that on the set, despite the extreme pressures she sometimes faced, especially from temperamental movie stars and actors, it was important that people not see her cry.

Resourceful women like her, discovered plenty of other tools they could use, that are generally not available to men.

For example, a senior executive at a major aerospace company — the only woman among eight senior execs — told me, she loved wearing a red dress whenever she knew she was going into tough negotiations with top management. People knew not to mess with Kathleen during her 'red-dress' days, as she called them.

So women can be tremendously effective, especially when they negotiate with confidence.

Giving Women The Edge...
For Some Men That's Complicated

But how do we develop confidence in a woman (and a daughter)?

There are two important ways.

First, dads who are involved with their kids, especially from a young age, tend to have kids that do better in school, and later in life.

But that's not all.

A landmark study of colleges found that women who were encouraged to express their opinions as children, tended to be more confident in expressing their opinions in school and throughout their lives – even when those opinions diverged from everyone else's.[10]

Being comfortable expressing your opinion is an essential tool of leadership and success, for both women and men.

So, can a father be confident enough to encourage his daughter to express her own unique opinion, even when it's different from his?

This can be tough for some men.

But a man who can periodically be willing to 'agree-to-disagree' with his daughter and be okay with that, can more easily plant seeds of confidence that will last a lifetime, with most women?

The good news for women is, regardless of what happened during your childhood, there are now many resources that were not available to previous generations.

Perhaps the greatest is the access to mentors. As more women are reaching senior positions throughout our society, it's becoming easier to find great female mentors who model self-confidence, while demonstrating the new 'rules of the game.'

Still, the power of a strong father-daughter relationship in building confidence and self-esteem in a woman cannot be overstated. And that's where this book can help.

Should We Be Turning Men Into Women... And Women Into Men

So, what have we learned?

For starters, women tend to be more emotionally sensitive than men. This can be a curse, but also a blessing. Along with this, women will tend to be self-critical and susceptible to feelings of rejection, but can also be ultra-aware of people's emotions, better than men in many cases.

Also, developing confidence, especially in young women, can have life-long benefits for them.

However, perhaps the greatest lesson in all this is, positive traits exist in both men and women. If we were to design the perfect human being, it might be a hybrid, somewhere between a man's toughness and a woman's sensitivity.

Of course, we are not trying to turn men into women, and women into men.

But if we could develop in a woman the strength to defend herself in a tough world, combined with the emotional sensitivity to understand what others are feeling, we will have given her a great advantage on the path to success and happiness in life.

That's why this book was created... to help open new doors of understanding about a subject that's rarely discussed – the impact of the father-daughter relationship on both men and women.

As you read the pages that follow, our hope is that you will be enlightened in ways that will bring even greater happiness, that you may not have expected.

References

1. Are Women More Emotional Than Men, by David P. Schmitt, PhD, Psychology Today, April 10, 2015

2. How to talk to a man; How to talk to a woman, by Robert Taibbi, L.C.S.W, Psychology Today, Nov. 10, 2012

3. Women And Money: Why They Avoid Risk And Lack Confidence When Making Decisions, by Eve Kaplan, CFP®, Forbes, Nov. 20, 2012

4. Statistics Have Become Suspect in Sex Discrimination Cases, by Tamar Lewin, The New York Times, Feb. 9, 1986

5. Fatality Facts – Men More Dangerous, General Statistics 2015, Insurance Institute for Highway Safety, http://www.iihs.org/iihs/topics/t/general-statistics/fatalityfacts/gender

6. Why Women Don't Negotiate Their Job Offers, by Hannah Riley Bowles, Harvard Business Review, June 19, 2014

7. Why Women Don't Apply For Jobs Unless They're 100% Qualified, by Tara Sophia Mohr, Harvard Business Review, Aug. 25, 2014

8. 3 Ways You Can Help Close the Pay Gap Now, by Zoe Henry, Inc Magazine, April 14, 2015

9. 10 Things Sheryl Sandberg Gets Exactly Right In 'Lean In,' by Susan Adams, Forbes, March 4, 2013

10. The father-daughter relationship: familial interactions that impact a daughter's style of life (referring to psychological work by Sophie Freud/1988 and Secunda 1992), by Rose Merlino Perkins, College Student Journal, Dec. 2001, Volume 35

Does Having a Daughter Change a Man?

There's a great line in the Steve Jobs movie, where his daughter asks why he behaved so badly during her early years, when he pretended he was NOT her father. In embarrassment, his response was simply, "I'm poorly made. "[1]

Poorly made or not, there's plenty of evidence that men change once they have a daughter.

Of course, not every man is affected in the same way. But often, when a man has a daughter, he suddenly cares how women are treated, in the workplace and in society.

She's the only ONE who can change him

This 'pro-woman' effect is especially evident with men in positions of power and influence.

Take the U.S. Supreme Court.

A study by Maya Sen, a professor at the University of Rochester, and Adam Glynn, a professor at Harvard University, uncovered a surprising fact... that male Justices tended to make more woman-friendly decisions than other men, once they had a daughter.[2]

A telling example is Justice Harry Blackmun.

A staunch conservative and opponent of women's rights when he was appointed to the Supreme Court by President Richard Nixon, Blackmun eventually became one of the most liberal justices on the Court.[3] [4]

What caused such a dramatic shift in his political ideology?

It was his daughter Sally. Once she was old enough to have deep discussions with her dad, his decisions began to shift more heavily towards women's rights.

In fact, Justice Blackmun became the deciding vote in the landmark Roe vs. Wade Supreme Court decision that legalized abortions in America... because of his daughter. His decision evolved, in a large part, from his deep discussions with Sally, who had previously struggled with the question of whether she herself should have an abortion.[4] [5] [6]

Had Justice Blackmun NOT had a daughter, would his decisions have been different?

So Stubborn...
Only A Daughter Could Change Him

Of course, Justice Blackmun wasn't the only powerful man affected by his daughter.

Women might never have won the right to vote without daughters putting pressure on their fathers.

Champ Clark, Speaker of the U.S. House of Representatives, guided his Democrat party to the eventual passage of the 19th amendment – granting women the right to vote in 1920 – in support of his suffragette daughter Genevieve, whom he adored.[7] [8]

When Genevieve was asked if she was surprised by her dad speaking in favor of giving women the right to vote, she confidently explained, "He would not have dared to come home if he had not."[9]

Britain's Prime Minister, Winston Churchill was another powerful man affected by his daughter.

For much of his early life, Churchill had been strongly opposed to giving women the right to vote in Britain. At one point he famously proclaimed, "...if we allow women to vote, it will mean the loss of social structure and the rise of every liberal cause under the sun. Women are [already] well represented by their fathers, brothers, and husbands."[10] [11]

This immovable stance against women's rights did not win Churchill friends among the masses of women suffragettes in Britain.[12]

But later in his life, after extensive discussions with his daughter Mary, he finally became convinced otherwise, and eventually supported and advocated for women to gain the right to vote.[13] [14]

Who besides a daughter could have convinced the stubborn Churchill to change his vote?

Another politician whose opinion was changed by his daughter was U.S. Vice President Dick Cheney, under President George W. Bush. Mostly in support of his gay daughter Mary, Cheney famously supported gay marriage against his Republican party's hard line on the topic.[15] [16]

So yes, there are plenty of examples of daughters having had tremendous influence over their famous and powerful fathers.

How About U.S. Presidents...

Few people realize that every U.S. President over the past 50 years, since Eisenhower, has been the father of at least one daughter while in the White House.

This may help explain why women's rights and protections in America have soared during the same period.

Take President Barack Obama.

He became an enthusiastic advocate for the rights of women and girls, as demonstrated through his creation of the Council of Women and Girls, for example.[17]

His rhetoric mirrored his advocacy, as he famously proclaimed, "We must carry forward the work of the women who came before us **and ensure our daughters have no limits** on their dreams, no obstacle to their achievements and no remaining ceilings to shatter."[18]

Would President Obama have been such an enthusiastic advocate, had his daughters Sasha and Malia not been with him in the White House?

How about President Donald Trump?

How different would Trump have been without his daughter Ivanka?

After all, is it a coincidence that shortly after Ivanka's birth, Trump started promoting women to higher positions within his company?

One of his high-profile promotions was for Barbara Res, who became the highest ranking woman in New York construction under Trump. He had her managing the construction of Trump Tower at a time when almost no women had senior construction positions.[19]

In 1989, Savvy Woman magazine featured Trump on the cover, with Barbara Res and two other women on his team with the headline, "Surprise! Mr. Macho's Inner Circle Isn't An All-Boys' Club."[20]

In his run for the White House, Trump's Campaign Manager Kellyanne Conway became the first woman in U.S. politics to win a Presidential campaign.[21] During his campaign, she was arguably the most influential of his advisors, and the one person who may have been responsible for his winning the White House.[22]

So, did having a daughter make Trump even more receptive to working with women?

Moreover, does daughter Ivanka wield more influence over her dad than her brothers do?

After all, before he became President, she was Executive Vice President over her father's company, The Trump Organization. In the White House, she has been the only one of his children taking residence there, and the only one appointed as Senior Advisor to the President of the United States by her father.[23] She's the only one of his children espousing policy for Trump, especially regarding women's empowerment and making child care more affordable.[24]

Who knows what Trump would have been like without a daughter. But there's evidence he would have been very different.

The Civil Rights Of Fatherhood

How about Dr. Martin Luther King, Jr.?

Most of us think of Dr. King as the iconic Civil Rights leader who changed the world. Yet this two-dimensional image only gives us a slice of what he was really like.

Had you asked his eldest child – daughter Yolanda – what her 'daddy' was like, you would have heard something very different.

She recalled with joy, a father who taught her how to swim when she was four, and how to ride a bike.

She remembered her 'daddy' rolling on the floor with her and her younger siblings until they drove their momma crazy. Momma would yell, "Stop... you're going to break something." So they'd wait until she was gone, and then go right back to rolling on the floor with daddy.[25]

She recalled her daddy always making them laugh. He even joked at the dinner table that he would die before he turned forty. She was twelve when he was killed.[26]

The Dr. King that she knew was a "buddy daddy," according to her, who didn't dwell on work when he was home. "He was my best friend," she explained.[27] He even took her to the amusement park, where they would ride the roller coaster, "screaming and giggling."[28]

"Of all the things daddy and I did together, traveling with him was my favorite," she explained.[29] In fact, from these trips together, she recalled one of the most important lessons her daddy taught her.

As she told it, on one of their trips, they were hand-in-hand in an airport waiting for a plane. Daddy stopped to buy a newspaper, and she silently slipped a candy bar into her purse. As they boarded the plane, when 'daddy' realized what she had done, he scolded her and in-no-uncertain-terms explained that upon their return flight, she would have to return the bar to the store, that stealing was wrong.[29]

Is this the Rev. Dr. Martin Luther King Jr. that we all think we know?

Is it any wonder that this icon of American history would reference his kids in such a profound way, in his most famous of speeches...

"I have a dream that my four little children will one day live in a nation where they will not be judged by the color of their skin, but by the content of their character. I have a dream today!"[30]

To what extent his daughter Yolanda influenced him, perhaps we will never fully understand.

But...

Is it a coincidence that Dr. King transformed himself from Baptist minister to Civil Rights leader, only after the birth of his daughter, their first child?

Is it a coincidence that 'daddy' became even more embroiled into Civil Rights activism, as his daughter grew old enough to travel with him, and to become a much more interactive part of his life?

Women Profoundly Change Their Dads... Even Without Realizing It

As with Dr. King, we often define a man simply by his beliefs and his actions. But the influence of a daughter cannot be overstated.

A 2011 study of 6,000 Danish companies further validates this.

What they discovered was, those companies run by men who had at least one daughter, tended to give women better pay and greater opportunities than companies run by men who didn't have a daughter.

Moreover, shortly after a daughter was born, men actually tended to increase pay and opportunities for women at their companies, more than at any other time.[31]

Going even further, a study published in Harvard Business Review explained that major U.S. companies "...run by male executives with female children, rated higher for diversity, employee relations and eco-friendliness. "[32]

The theory proposed by its authors, Henrik Cronqvist, a professor at University of Miami's business school, and China Europe International Business School professor Frank Yu, is interesting.

They believe "...the effect, known as the 'female socialization hypothesis' has been shown to prompt fathers to adopt some of their daughters' values and thinking."[32]

Therefore, it shouldn't be a surprise that media titans Rupert Murdoch[33] (Fox-TV and Films, The Wall Street Journal) and Sumner Redstone[34] (CBS-TV, Paramount Pictures) both lobbied for their daughters to run their media empires, despite having sons.

So yes, whether a man is famous or not, having a daughter could change him more profoundly than many of us may realize.

The Drug Dealer And The Attorney...

Our own experiences with The Father-Daughter Project™ support this idea that men are changed once they have a daughter.

In our interviews for this book, one of the most powerful attorneys in the nation and an ex-drug-dealer, both had no hesitation explaining the impact their daughters have had on them.

The attorney told us, "...there's nothing more humbling than a 3-year-old with her hands on her hips, telling you, 'You are a mean person.' " "I scolded her," he said, "for saying such a thing, but she retorted," 'Someone has to tell you, because everyone's afraid of you.'

The next day, he asked his secretary if she thought he was a mean person.

Her response floored him. She leaned across her desk and whispered, "Do you want the truth?"

This is an example of how a seemingly simple comment from a young daughter could have such an overwhelming impact on a man. He told us that her comment combined with his secretary's response, got him to reexamine how he interacted with everyone in his 100-person law firm... all because he didn't want his daughter to think badly of her daddy.

Similarly, the ex-drug dealer we interviewed explained that, as he held his newborn daughter in his arms for the first time, he suddenly became overwhelmed with fear. Would his little girl grow up ashamed of her daddy, once she realized what he did for a living?

"At that very moment, I decided to give up drugs and alcohol, and go to work for my dad. I'd never before had someone I cared about, who'd be watching me so closely. I just couldn't bear her growing up ashamed of me."

Of Course... All Men Are Not Created Equal

The point here is simple. Whether famous or not, a man can be profoundly affected by his daughter.

Sure, not every father or every daughter will be affected positively. But given half a chance, a surprising number of men will respond in ways that enrich both the dad and the daughter, and perhaps, even the people around them.

That's why this book was created in the first place.

Our hope is that somewhere between great and terrible dads, you will discover a man who has been deeply affected by his daughter.

Hopefully, in the pages that follow, you will begin to understand MEN – starting with your own father – in a way that you may not have expected.

And for the men reading this book, hearing from real fathers in ways that men rarely share with others, our hope is that you will find inspiration and guidance on how to strengthen your relationship with the one person who will remain your daughter... til death do you part.

Enjoy!

References

1. IMDB – Steve Jobs (2015)

2. Why Men With Daughters May Be The Key To Closing The Gender Wage Gap, by Lisa Evans, Fast Company June 30, 2014

3. What Work / Gender Equality, by Iris Bohnet, Harvard University Press 2016,

4. Justice Blackmun, Author of Abortion Right, Dies, by Linda Greenhouse, The New York Times, March 5, 1999

5. Daughter of Justice Blackmun Goes Public about Roe, by Cynthia L. Cooper, Women's eNews, February 29, 2004

6. Harry Blackmun's daughter speaks about her father's Roe v. Wade deci-sion, by Sally Terzo, National Right to Life News Today, March 9, 2016

7. James Beauchamp ("Champ") Clark, The State Historical Society of Missouri

8. Genevieve Clark Thompson, The Champ Clark House (Historical Society of Missouri)

9. Clark Declares for Suffrage, The New York Times, June 28, 1914

10. AZ Quotes

11. Churchill's "Infallibility": Myth on Myth, by Richard M. Langworth (Churchill Historian), July 10, 2012

12. Winston vs. the Women, by Sarah Gristwood, Huffington Post, Sept. 30, 2015

13. Churchill the Wartime Feminist, by Andrew Roberts, The International Churchill Society, Bulletin #48, June 2012

14. An Interview with Mary Soames - "Father Always Came First, Second And Third," The International Churchill Society, Autumn 2002

15. High-Profile Politicians Who Changed Their Positions on Gay Marriage, by Alisa Wiersema, ABC News, March 15, 2013

16. Dick Cheney Actively Supports Gay Marriage in Non Campaign Years, by Philip Bump, The Atlantic, Nov. 18, 2013

17. Obama's Council on Women and Girls, by Lisa Belkin, The New York Times, March 11, 2009

18. Presidential Proclamation--Women's History Month, 2011, The White House, Feb. 28, 2011

19. The Frontline Interview: Barbara Res, PBS, Sept. 27, 2016

20. Donald Trump, a champion of women? His female employees think so, By Frances Stead Sellers, Washington Post, November 24, 2015

21. Conway shatters glass ceiling as first woman to run a successful presidential campaign, by Gabby Morrongiello, Washington Examiner, Nov. 10, 2016

22. Why Donald Trump Picked Kellyanne Conway to Manage his Campaign, by Alex Altman and Zeke J. Miller, Time Magazine, Aug. 22, 2016

23. Ivanka Trump, Shifting Plans, Will Become a Federal Employee, by Maggie Haberman and Rachel Abrams, The New York Times, March 29, 2017

24. Ivanka Trump quietly settles into White House life, by Betsy Klein, CNN, February 9, 2017

25. To Her, Rev. King Was Simply Dad, by Roger Simon, Chicago Tribune, January 14, 1985\

26. Yolanda King Recalls Father As Two Men There Was A Civil Rights Leaders And 'Daddy', by Virginia De Leon, The Spokesman-Review, Jan. 31, 1997

27. Yolanda King's father was her buddy, The Blade, Jan. 28, 2005

28. Yolanda King says memories of father are full of love, laughter, Cleveland-19 News, Associated Press, 2005

29. Wichita Storyteller Remembers Yolanda King's "Daddy" On Anniversary Of Birthday, by Carla Eckels, KMUW – Wichita 89.1 – Wichita's NPR Station, Jan. 15, 2016

30. "I Have a Dream," Address delivered at the March on Washington for Jobs and Freedom, (Aug. 28, 1963), Stanford University – The Martin Luther King, Jr. Research and Education Institute

31. Why Men With Daughters May Be The Key To Closing The Gender Wage Gap, by Lisa Evans, Fast Company June 30, 2014

32. CEOs with daughters run more socially responsible companies, research finds, by Jena McGregor, Washington Post, Oct. 26, 2015

33. The Heiress – The Rise of Elisabeth Murdoch, by Ken Auletta, The New Yorker, Dec. 10, 2012

34. Shari Redstone, Viacom heir apparent to an ailing empire, by Matthew Garrahan, Financial Times, May 27, 2016

Do You Ever Wonder What *Really* Goes On in a Father's Mind?

Voices From Within This Book

HURTING ON THE INSIDE

"One thing my daughter doesn't know about me or understand is what I went through as a kid...how I had a dad who didn't love me, at least didn't love me the way that I understood... and a mom who was vacant. [I don't think my daughter] knows or understands the wounds I have from that."

BEING NEEDED

"I love being needed [even though it may be because of my daughter's illness]... I don't think she's ever needed me before. I'm very happy to be [there for her now], anyway that she needs me."

HOW MY DAUGHTER HAS AFFECTED ME

"She has made me laugh. She has made me cry. She's affected all of my emotions. She's probably pulled on every emotional heart string. But [in doing that] she showed me the tender softer side of myself.

This is a hard question for me... what I've learned by being her father...

I've just learned to be caring [and] love unconditionally. Yeah, that's where I am."

This book contains excerpts from personal interviews with 101 fathers of daughters, telling us...

... I wish my daughter *really* knew what it means to me to be her father.

Why The Father-Daughter Project™ Was Created

When she was twenty-two years old, I mentioned to my daughter Lauren, "Now that you're grown up I suddenly realize, I don't really know you."

Tears slowly formed in the sides of her eyes, and she lowered her head to avoid looking directly at me. Then she whispered to me, "I've been waiting my whole life to hear that."

I was stunned by her comment. Uncontrollably, tears streamed down my face as if a faucet had opened. I could not control the burst of sadness I felt. I was overcome with an emotion I had not felt ever in my life.

Over the days and months that followed, I was troubled about this seemingly failed relationship with my own daughter. Despite decades as a psychology and human behavior specialist, I realized that in some ways I was clueless about the connection with my own daughter.

In a way, deep down I was not fully sure what I was feeling, this strange emotion of profound sadness combined with confusion. How could this have happened? How could something so simple feel so difficult—having a close connection to one of the most important people in my life?

The Father-Daughter Project began as a way to learn the experiences of other fathers with daughters—directly from them.

I wondered if other dads with daughters struggled with the complexity of the relationship between a father and his daughter as I had with my daughter Lauren. After all, my relationship with my son was easy. I got him. I understood what he was going through. But with my daughter… there was something profoundly different.

101 dads graciously came forward to share their own personal stories, on recorded telephone interviews. They came from almost all fifty states and Canada, ranging in age from their twenties to their eighties. They were straight or gay, married, divorce or widowed, of almost every race and economic situation. They were similar and different from each other in numerous ways. But the two things they all had in common were, they were the father of at least one daughter and they were willing to share their stories.

This book is a compilation from these interviews with 101 fathers—in their own words (with periodic brief comments from me). Some of their comments and observations were incredibly funny, some were deeply sad, but all were real.

What I gained from their words was profound beyond my wildest expectations, so this book is my opportunity to share these words and interviews with you. I hope you enjoy them as I have.

James I. Bond
Father of a thirty-one year old Son and three Daughters
age twenty-seven, twenty-six and twenty
(I am a father-in-training)
Founder, The Father-Daughter Project™

Observations from 101 Fathers of Daughters

This book is based on our interviews with 101 fathers with daughters.

The dads included in this book are not perfect. But somehow, in the words and stories they share, hopefully you will find some wisdom that may help you understand this complex relationship between fathers and daughters.

Why Focus on Daughters... Aren't Sons Also Important?

To most dads, daughters are very different than sons.

The brain of a dad and his son are physically similar. Dads were once boys, and so a dad can generally relate more easily to a son's experience of growing up than he can to the experience of a daughter growing up.

For a girl, the parts of her brain that manage emotion and communication can be significantly different than those in the brain of her dad and of men. These differences lead many dads to a feeling of emotional disconnection when trying to interact with his young developing daughter.

While many dads overcome this feeling of awkwardness and detachment by opening themselves up emotionally to interaction with their daughters, some find the chasm so great that it becomes a barrier that subtly keeps them distant from their daughters.

Numerous dads have told us their connection with their daughter has become one of the most important relationships in their life—if not the most important—while others have described a relationship of discomfort and distance with a daughter they only partially know.

In part this happens because an open relationship with a daughter can expose a man to his sensitive, nurturing, emotional side – in ways that may feel threatening to his definition of what a man is. At a primal level it may feel dangerous.

So this book was created to help daughters better understand the father-daughter relationship—from a father's perspective. In this way, the words and voices throughout this book may help you in strengthening what could be one of your most important lifelong relationships.

For the men and dads who read this book, hopefully the stories and insights will strike a chord with you about the complicated, wonderful relationship that can exist between a father and his daughter.

THE TEN STAGES OF THE FATHER-DAUGHTER EXPERIENCE

Of course, every daughter and every dad is different.
These are very general guidelines.

STAGE	AGE	A DAUGHTER'S EXPERIENCE	A DAD'S EXPERIENCE
One	Birth	Connection—new life and family	• Dad holds the tiny defenseless child
Two	0-2	Awareness—She learns to walk, talk and interact	• She falls asleep on dad • Dad's first conversations with her
Three	2	Assertiveness—She learns to say No	• Dad deals with her contrary behavior
Four	2-5	Socialization—She learns how to act in public	• Dad plays with her • Dad (and mom) teach her how to behave
Five	5-12	School—She fits in, learns the rules	• Dad may help her adjust and survive (homework, sports, tutor, vacation, etc)
Six	12-16	Peers—She establishes her personality as distinct from her parents	• Dad (and mom) give her more freedom • Dad (and/or mom) initially discuss sex
Seven	16-18	Driving—She has freedom and new responsibility	• Dad may interact with her friends • Dad (and mom) may set boundaries
Eight	18-25	Independence—She is introduced to living away from home	• Dad may be there for her if she needs him • Dad may have long discussions with her
Nine	25-49	Distance—She has an independent life and may have a family	• Dad interacts mostly by phone and Internet • Dad periodically visits
Ten	Over 49	Maturity—She has a some-what established life	• Dad has discussions with her about life and family

On Being a Father to a Daughter

This chapter provides a glimpse
into the emotional experience
of being a father
to a daughter.

It also considers the impact
of a dad's own parents
and his comfort
with women in general
in understanding
what has molded him
into the kind of father
he has become.

Inside this Chapter

Observations from 101 Dads of Daughters

- My Daughter Was A Real Mystery To Me
- I'm Nervous Around Females
- I Found Daughters More Complex Than Sons
- Girls Get Treated Differently Than Boys

- I Gained A Lot From Having A Daughter
- It Was Surprising How Much My Own Parents Affected Me
- I Wish I Had Known My Grandparents
- There's A Difference Between A Great Dad And A Lousy Dad

- A Daughter's Relationship With Mom Is Different Than With Dad
- I Struggled To Find The Time I Needed To Be A Good Father
- Being A Divorced Dad Was Tough At Times
- I Really Enjoy Being A Stepfather

- Although They Have Similarities—Every Child Is Different
- One Daughter Is Easier To Talk To Than The Other
- I Had Fear And Resentment At Being Such A Young Father
- Being A Father Is The Most Incredible Thing In My Life

My Daughter Was A Real Mystery To Me

Girls Were Aliens, A Breed Apart—I Had To Rethink How To Be A Parent

"I grew up in a household with two brothers, so to me girls were aliens.

As a young man I had to learn through dating what they were like. I didn't have any girls to interact with growing up, so they were just a whole breed apart from me.

With [my son], I knew I was right because I was a boy at one time so I know what's going on in your head. But I didn't know what was going on in [my daughter's] head, so I had to slooooooow down and think.

I had to think much more with her. I had to learn how to be a daddy a little different. A lot different. Because I wasn't sure all the time what's right with her.

You tell your kid to do something, hopefully you're sure you're right. If you're not, you're going to have to slow down and parent differently."

Ken, 9/11 New York City fireman and father of a six year old daughter and two sons

I Wasn't Prepared For How Emotional Females Are

"I have two brothers that I grew up with.

I think not having any sisters growing up made girls kind of a mystery, you know what I mean. They're more emotional—as I find most women are than men."

Ed, fifty-one year old father to a fifteen year old daughter and two sons

My Daughter's Been A Mystery And A Gift—She's Made Me More Open

"She's been a female presence in my life that has been both a mystery and a gift. It's just been a delight to see her grow.

4

[If I never had a daughter] I don't think my heart would be as open. I think I would have gone more towards [being] a macho male. More testosteronic."

George, seventy-five year old father of fifty-two year old daughter and two sons; also later became stepfather of another daughter (when she was a teenager) and a stepson

I Would Definitely Be More Intuitive Raising A Son Than A Daughter

"I think that I would feel innately more intuitive with a son because I know what it's like to be a little boy, having been there. However, never having been a little girl, it really requires a different mindset.

I would assume the responsibility and the desire to care for my child is one in the same whether it be a boy or a girl. However, the relation in terms of understanding a little boy or a little girl, I think that probably is a little different."

Ray, forty-eight year old computer executive, father of a five year old daughter

To better understand the dads, we also asked how they are around females in general.

I'm Nervous Around Females

I'm Intimidated By Women—I Don't Understand The Rules Of Engagement

> It was surprising how many dads said they were nervous around women.
>
> For some this discomfort seemed to carry forward into their relationship with their daughter.

"Women intimidate me. I have some fear around women.

I mean, I've built my image in a man's world, so it's a lot easier for me to understand the rules of engagement. And I've been pretty successful at it.

Whereas with women—I mean, I've been successful dating and doing all those things. But it's always been an acquisition for me versus actually functioning in their world."

Bill, forty-eight year old father of a twenty-year-old daughter and a twenty-four year old son

I'm On Eggshells Around Women

"I think I have a long standing fear of women. In particular I fear that I will too readily and unconsciously give up my power to women.

So on a certain level, there is just a low grade fear that causes me to be on eggshells around women. I don't feel threatened in the same way by men at all."

John, fifty-six year old schoolteacher, divorced father of eighteen year old daughter (divorced when his daughter was seven but remained close to her)

I Found Daughters More Complex Than Sons

Daughters Require More Patience Than A Son Would

"Daughters I think, are a bit more complex than sons. Daughters in a lot of ways require a bit more patience, a bit more understanding from a male point of view.

You know, relating to a girl who then becomes a young woman. I think it's a bit more challenging for a father to really understand all the things that a daughter is going through as she matures.

In relationships [and] in friendships, I think one tends to understand his gender a bit better. You can relate. You've been there. You've seen it. You've felt all those feelings. Or [at least], you can certainly put yourself in that person's shoes.

But with the women you're guessing. Sometimes you guess right, sometimes you guess wrong. You try to keep notes so that you learn along the way."

Bill, forty-six year old human resources manager of a Fortune 500 company, with a twenty-six year old stepdaughter and a twenty one year old son. He came into his step-daughter's life when she was two.

Daughters Want You To Speak And Sing To Them

"You can start to see right away [when they're babies], that there's a difference between the boys and the girls—how much they like to be close, right up to your face, touching your face all the time.

The boys were more distant and observant and looking around and seeing the world. The girl always wanted to be staring into your eyes. She always wanted to be touching your face and to be held and to be whispered to and sang to."

Ken, 9/11 New York City fireman and father of a six year old daughter and two sons

Daughters Are More Sensitive Emotionally Than Sons

"Actually, my daughters are so different {from each other} too. {But yeah, daughters} are softer, meaning they're just *not* as rough and tumble.

I also say, they're much more sensitive emotionally. And that may be more about how my son's already getting socialized by people and the changes {my kids} are already going through."

Ron, forty-seven year old school counselor and father of an eleven-year-old daughter and a twin eight-year-old daughter and son

Girls Are Less Physically Aggressive

"I'm a school teacher, so I'd seen classrooms with a majority of girls and classrooms with the majority of boys, and the atmosphere is different. There's a level of assertiveness, of aggression,

[but] with the girls less so. Not less competitive, but in my experience, less of a physical expression of that [aggression]."

Andrew, forty-six year old schoolteacher, father of two daughters age nine and ten

Daughters Are More Up And Down—But Easier To Connect With Emotionally

"[Girls], they're different, okay. Much more emotional, much more up and down. Yet at the same time, more open and caring.

My relationship with [my stepdaughter] Tiffany has developed into one that is much closer today. We're much closer than I am with either of my own two sons or with my stepson—just because we talk so much and we're on the same level."

Terry, sixty-two year old engineer and father of two sons age thirty-eight and thirty-four, a stepson age twenty-four and a twenty-one year old stepdaughter

It's Primal—Women Are Better Communicators Than Men

"Oh absolutely, women are different than men. We [men] think different.

It's tough to not be on generalities. I'll try to avoid that, but in my experience, daughters are much more intuitive, more aware, and they connect more [emotionally] at an earlier age.

Although with [my stepdaughter] Susan, of course I didn't know her as a small child. But even now, I see the difference between the [girls'] biological brothers and themselves. It's dramatic.

Men or boys are the providers. They're involved in their work. Women are the socializers. You know, the primal instincts which I believe are so much of our heritage, [with] the women sitting around the camp fire and working hard while the men were off hunting.

So the women developed their communication, talking, connecting across the fire or whatever it was while the men were off hunting or killing or protecting the tribe. I see that heritage almost every day in {my} daughters."

Red, seventy-eight year old father of forty-nine year old daughter, three sons, three step sons and a fifty-year-old stepdaughter (his stepdaughter was eighteen when he came into her life)

Women Have A Different Kind Of Strength Than Men

"The awareness of their strength was something that was not shown to me or taught to me when I was growing up.

So therefore, the way I treat my daughter or the women in my life is, in some respects like the weaker vessel. Although I'm finding out that they have their own strength."

Donnie, fifty-six year old father of a thirty-two year old daughter and thirty year old son (divorced when his daughter was eight but remained close to her)

As A Father Your Defenses Are Down—So It's Easier To See How Girls Are Different

"Men and women aren't the same. We're different. We think different. We feel different. We have different tolerances. The way women think about things is just so different from the way we think about things.

> What does that mean: "Your defenses are down when you have a daughter?"
>
> Several dads explained that it's about being vulnerable...
>
> It's about knowing that your little girl is always watching you.

When you have a daughter, all your defenses are down so you can see it and you can feel it and understand it. There's no barriers to that knowledge now because it's being given to you in such an innocent way."

Ken, 9/11 New York City fireman and father of a six year old daughter and two sons

Girls Get Treated Differently Than Boys

I Realized My Daughter Was Going To Grow Up To Become A Woman

> "Daughters are an entirely different creation than sons in regards to their makeup and their needs and their… 'giftings.' They're just a different thing altogether.
>
> I treat [my daughter] in a way different than my sons. I treat my sons in a more, for lack of a better term, rough and tumble, [but] her—not in a soft and gentle way. [Instead] I respond to her as a woman. I mean, when she was younger it was in anticipation of the fact that she was going to grow up [into a woman]."
>
> *Richard, fifty year old father of a twenty-five year old daughter and two sons*

Girls Act Like Girls And Boys Act Like Boys—So They Get Treated Differently

> "[Daughters] interact differently, and they get treated differently. They can change the room just by walking into it.
>
> The boys know that [my daughter] gets treated differently. I have to explain to them, it's not better or worse. It's just different.
>
> It's just that she's a girl and she acts like a girl, and you're a boy and you act like a boy. You get treated the way you act and girls get treated the way they act.
>
> [Girls and boys have] different emotional tolerances and so, everybody does not get treated the same. The world is not fair and—not necessarily good or bad, it's just the way it is."
>
> *Ken, 9/11 New York City fireman and father of a six year old daughter and two sons*

I Gained A Lot From Having A Daughter

It Was More Than I Expected—I Grew So Much By Being Her Dad

> "Yeah, it was definitely not what I expected but much better than I expected. Because I got so much more out of it. I grew so much by being her dad."

> *Ken, 9/11 New York City fireman and father of a six year old daughter and two sons*

My Daughter Got Me to Experience Things I Would Otherwise Have Missed

> "My youngest daughter has given me a chance to connect on various interests I would have missed out on, [like the] physical affection and nurturing.

> That's more difficult for my son. I have to really push to get it [from him]. It's amazing how that doesn't happen [with him] because I'm a very affectionate expressive person.

> [Also] I would never have gotten to play 'pretty, pretty princess' {he laughs}. Hey I had a lot of fun battling to get the crown. Gotta love getting the crown. Get that tiara in your hair. That's kind of what jumps out to me."

> *Ron, forty-seven year old school counselor and father of an eleven-year-old daughter and a twin eight-year-old daughter and son*

I Talk About Different Things With My Daughter Than With My Son

> "I think women in general process things a little bit differently. The kinds of things I share with my daughter are different than what I share with my son, even though I consider we all have a very open relationship.

> Interesting enough, my daughter is probably in some ways more like me and my son is probably in some ways more like his mother. So there are just some different dynamics in general with fathers

and daughters. Different dynamics that take place specifically in our relationships."

David, sixty-three year old real estate appraiser and Vietnam vet, father of a thirty-seven year old son and a twenty-nine year old daughter (divorced when his daughter was eight but stayed very engaged with his children growing up)

Having A Daughter Helped Me Understand Women A Little Better

"[If my daughter had never been part of my life], I wouldn't be able to understand women as much as I do now.

Not that I have a great understanding by any stretch of the imagination. But just to see how different they are as human beings, you know, [how different my daughter is] from her brothers...

She's given me a whole new way to love. She's given me a whole new way of feeling—

Many dads hadn't realized how much they gained from having their daughter.

Several explained that spending time with her *slowed* them down and got them to listen better... without their mind racing to what they wanted to say next.

that a girl's love is different than a boy's love. {He chokes up} She taught me how to love in a whole new way. In a softer gentler way. In a slower more understanding way. I had to go slower."

Ken, 9/11 New York City fireman and father of a six year old daughter and two sons

It Was Surprising How Much My Own Parents Affected Me

I Was Going To Be A Better Father Than My Dad Was

"…I was going to be the father that I didn't know, that I missed as a child…"

Andrew, forty-six year old schoolteacher, father of two daughters age nine and ten

I Didn't Feel Loved As A Child—My Daughter Doesn't Know That

"One thing my daughter doesn't know about me or understand is what I went through as a kid, what I went through when I was her age and younger. How I had a dad that didn't love me, at least didn't love me the way that I understood. And how I had a mom who was vacant.

My daughter doesn't know or understand the wounds that I have from that. She doesn't know or understand all the work I've done to get to be the man I am now.

I don't need her to know or understand those things at all. I just need her to know and understand who I am now.

She's starting to get it. As she gets older she's starting to see who I am. She's starting to understand it, because she sees other men. She's smart enough to make a comparison."

Mark, forty-four year old Navy pilot, father of a fifteen year old daughter and an eleven year old son (divorced when his daughter was seven but stayed involved as a dad)

My Dad Never Shared His Feelings With His Kids

"Absolutely. Absolutely [I've shared my feelings with my younger daughter]. That's one of the big differences between how I do things and how my parents did. I'm very willing so share how I feel.

Like just the other day, I asked my youngest to do something really simple for me, as I was heading out the door, and she said 'No.' I expressed myself very clearly on how I felt about it. Not just the anger about it but the sadness and disappointment, that family takes care of each other.

[Still] I'm surprised how much I ended up being like my dad, in ways I didn't want. Very pleased in the ways I did want."

Ron, forty-seven year old school counselor and father of an eleven-year-old daughter and a twin eight-year-old daughter and son

I Loved My Father But I Wanted To Be A Different Kind Of Dad—Less Self-Centered

"I guess one of my issues about being a father was to make sure that I covered the bases that my father didn't cover.

I always loved my father very much, but I don't think he was such a terrific dad, much more self-centered. I think he learned to care more about himself than the family as a unit in some ways.

So I spent my whole life making sure that I did *not* do or act the way he did.

Notwithstanding that, I think that I was always a very good son and treated him in a very, very loving warm way. But, you know, I did learn from his negative [example] how to act as a dad in some ways, or how I thought a dad should be. And I think I'm getting a lot of returns for it.

I think my kids like me. I guess that's the other part. I truly believe that my kids—there's no question they love me, but I think my kids like me, and that's a pretty nice thing to say."

Len, sixty-eight year old attorney, father of a thirty-five year old son, a thirty-four year old daughter and a twenty-eight year old stepdaughter

Unlike My Dad—When I Make A Mistake I Go Back And Apologize

"My father would have never admitted a mistake. So I love that when I do something wrong, like yell at my daughter, I'm willing to go back and apologize, and then tell her that's not the way I want to be.

For many of these dads, admitting they weren't perfect suddenly meant they could be themselves around their daughters.

For some reason, relationships with sons seemed to be different.

[So having a daughter] has taught me how weak and how strong I am as a parent, [in a way] that I would have never predicted before.

I realize my need to be liked is much bigger than I wanted it to be. Yet with that, I'm surprised at how tough I can be when I need to be and want to be, [but] do it in a way that's not abusive in any way.

I don't think any of my kids question whether I really love them, which was the question I always had with my dad in the way he dealt with me. I'd be shocked [if my kids didn't know I love them]."

Ron, forty-seven year old school counselor and father of an eleven-year-old daughter and a twin eight-year-old daughter and son

My Father Was Emotionally Distant So I Didn't Get The Tools I Needed As A Dad

"I had collected a lot of my father's tendencies for not being very demonstrative in my emotions. So [as a father] I was fairly reserved as far as my expressions of my emotions.

My father really didn't know how to express his love. I don't recall him being a tender loving father. He was fairly distant, removed.

Looking back on [my dad] I don't think he really had good skills for any personal relations at that time, and he didn't know how to deal with expressing intimacy.

I was present with him in a lot of things, whether we were cutting wood or whatnot, but it was not a direct intentional 'mentoring' type relationship.

[So when I became a father] I didn't feel totally competent at how to relate to this young lady as she was growing up. I knew I should be doing this differently but I didn't have the tools to do it."

Richard, fifty year old male nurse anesthesiologist, father of a twenty-five year old daughter and two sons

Feeling Emotionally Incested By My Mother, I'm Cautious To Not Get Close To My Daughter

"My mom did not get her intimacy needs met in her relationship with her husband and therefore was extremely clingy with her children... In a sense I was emotionally incested by her.

... [So as a father] there's a part of me that doesn't feel like I particularly want to be my daughter's confidant. That's one of the things that my mother did with me, and I think it was not healthy."

John, fifty-six year old schoolteacher, divorced father of eighteen year old daughter (divorced when his daughter was seven but remained close to her)

Growing Up With An Abusive Father, I Became Determined To Be A Better Dad

"Well here's the thing. I didn't want my child to grow up without a dad. I grew up for the most part without a dad. Then when I did get a dad it was an abusive-as-hell dad. He was, you know, an alcoholic and rage-aholic and physically abusive. I mean, seriously physically abusive. And he was abusive to my mom too.

So I knew what I didn't want to be like. I didn't want to be an absentee guy. I needed to do the right thing."

Ray, forty-eight year old computer executive, father of a five year old daughter

I Wish I Had Known My Grandparents

I Lost A Lot Because I Didn't Know My Grandparents

"I wished my parents knew how to engage my own kids more. I think they would have gotten more out of them. It would be nice to have my kids think of my parents as fondly as I'm sure they do my in-laws.

I don't blame my parents. It's just who they are and how they were, and their own personal histories, and the fact that my in-laws are the most incredible in-laws and incredible grandparents.

One of the things around the sadness that my in-laws bring up, is how much I lost at not having grandparents [myself]. I never knew my grandparents. When I watch my kids with my in-laws, it really reinforces how much I lost."

Ron, forty-seven year old school counselor and father of an eleven-year-old daughter and a twin eight-year-old daughter and son

There's A Difference Between A Great Dad And A Lousy Dad

A Good Dad Doesn't Try To Buy His Kids' Love

"Wow, I guess a great dad, I believe, is somebody who's developed a relationship where they can talk to their kids about almost anything they want to talk about, and [is] not particularly judgmental.

I mean, I think being judgmental is what screws up relationships. So as much as I have my own beliefs, I do my best not to be judgmental [towards] what my kids are going through, and what they think about. Trying to be more understanding, which isn't so easy sometimes.

> That was a difficult question: "Do you feel you've been a *great* or a *lousy* dad?"
>
> Deep down that question unnerved some dads.
>
> That's why we started by asking them about *other* dads... a much easier question for many to answer.

I have friends that I think have basically tried to buy their relationships with their kids. I think they are lousy dads. I think they've been unbelievably overindulgent with their children. They didn't want to say 'no' because they were buying their [kids'] love. I think that makes for a crummy dad.

I think people that deal honestly with their kids and talk to them in a straightforward manner have a much better chance of success with their children."

Len, sixty-eight year old attorney, father of a thirty-five year old son, a thirty-four year old daughter and a twenty-eight year old stepdaughter

Fathers Today Are Much More Involved In Raising Their Kids Than In The Past

"My son and son-in-law are better fathers than I was. They are involved, they listen.

Fathers today are more involved from an early age and that's the secret.

I think they are more attentive to [their kids], more sensitive to them. I don't know where they learned that but I think that's the secret—paying attention to the kid, and [even the way they] discipline them, not physically but finding a way to do it more subtly.

It's important [today], I think, just being with your kids, talking to them, playing with them. Much more than I did, and much, much more than my father did.

I see that as a general rule with younger couples, that fathers are much more active and much more involved in the whole process of raising a child now than it used to be. Actually listening to the child and not commanding. Not being the super boss, but more reasoning with them than commanding.

I think they're more flexible and getting better results. It takes longer but they finally convinced me."

Leonard, seventy-three year old ex- school music teacher, father of a forty-six year old son and a thirty-three year old daughter (divorced later in life but has stayed close to his daughter)

A Great Dad Gives And Gets Lots Of Hugs

"In the early years, be willing to encourage and participate in the girlie things and don't worry about what it looks like. Some of my fondest moment memories were playing the game 'pretty-pretty-princess'.

Encourage them to connect with their emotions and their nurturing side because it's their strength typically. Don't worry about rough housing with them. They need it. Don't assume that they're gonna be girly. They may not, and that's okay.

Bless them and love them constantly. Affirm them a lot and be their strength. Even if they get angry at you for being it, always be their strength. They need something that they know they can count on for safety and protection.

So if you gotta be tough with them, be tough. But never let them doubt that you love them. That is what I'm saying. Show and get lots of hugs. That would be very good."

Ron, forty-seven year old school counselor and father of an eleven-year-old daughter and a twin eight-year-old daughter and son

A Great Dad Can Just Listen Without Needing To Tell Her What To Do

"A great dad is listening, being there to accept your child without judgment, supporting them, listening and understanding their dreams and their aspirations.

A bad dad is, trying to force your own ideas and your own wishes upon your kid. A bad dad is making them into something that you want them to be rather than what they want.

A good dad is just being there. Sometimes just to listen and not to tell them what to do. A good dad is, at the same time, watching out for stuff that's really dangerous and could be poignant, but not focusing on the small stuff that doesn't make any difference."

Terry, sixty-two year old engineer and father of two sons age thirty-eight and thirty-four, a stepson age twenty-four and a twenty-one year old stepdaughter

Crying In Front Of Your Daughter Can Be A Show Of Strength

"I've tried not to hide anything from my daughter. There are times we've been having discussions and I've cried. I'm a firm believer that crying at the right time and place is a show of strength rather than weakness—that you're able to open yourself up."

Rob, forty-eight year old truck driver going to night school for massage therapy, father of a ten year old daughter and a twenty-three year old son (from a previous marriage who he also remains involved with)

A Good Dad Commits To Keeping The Marriage Together For His Kids

"One of my pet peeves is—I think fathers these days and men in general are way too willing to abandon their kids. It pains me because I've seen the effect it has on their kids. And it angers me that men are so blind to what we're doing to our kids.

> This came up a few times...
>
> To have a positive relationship with his daughter, a dad needed to move past his own personal problems.

[When we go through divorce] we just see from our perspectives and the women we are leaving, and we don't put the whole picture together.

What I'm also saying is that, when we choose to have kids, I believe we make an agreement with our kids that they will have two parents—that when we walk out of the marriage or allow the marriage to deteriorate where the women leave us, I believe we're breaking a solemn vow to our kids. It's one they have no choice over but I think will have a huge effect on their life.

So even if I'm a great dad, I should do everything I can to keep that marriage together. This idea of, 'I stay in the marriage because I love my wife and when the love's gone I need to leave,' it's ridiculous.

I have a brother-in-law who's in an arranged marriage. It wasn't about love, it was about something else. And their kids are incredible. It's a different way of looking at it.

I think in our modern day, we've made marriage all about love, and we've lost the part about commitment. I think commitment is the bigger thing. I think it's easier to have commitment and maintain that in a marriage than it is to maintain love in a marriage. And our kids need the commitment.

[So with me as her dad, my daughter] gets an impeccable role model. I'm all about my values and I don't just talk, I walk the talk. She's gonna get two parents unless one of us dies."

Ron, forty-seven year old school counselor and father of an eleven-year-old daughter and a twin eight-year-old daughter and son

A Good Dad Needs To Get Past His Own Problems—Then Everything Gets Better

"[I wasn't the best dad when my daughter was younger.] Personally at the time I had my own ripping bad issues with depression and dealing with alcohol and things like that. So I was not as present as I should have been.

I knew I should be doing this differently but I didn't have the tools to do it. So, I would be frustrated.

Not that there was ever anything where I was just totally out of hand. But it was more of me covering up my deep wounds and internalizing everything and withdrawing.

It wasn't like I was drunk all the time, that kind of thing. I wasn't one of those kind of guys that got DUIs and whatnot. I drank a fair amount but I'd still function well. I didn't lose my job.

But I would say the depression trumped about everything at the time and I was disappearing in my own way. So I would withdraw—because I didn't want to inflict my issues upon my family.

If I had to do it over again, it's so hard to say [what I would do] because at the time, my developmental level was such that I might not have been able to hear what I hear now. It was just my own maturing process.

I don't have a lot of regrets other than the fact that there were some things that I didn't experience with my kids that I should have as far as being present, because I was off in my own issues.

[However] I was very proactive in dealing with my own issues, through counseling, therapy, the whole nine yards. I mean, I knew that this was not right. Consciously I was saying, 'This is not [my family's] fault. They don't deserve to bear the brunt of this.'

— I Had To Push Past My Awkwardness To Spend Time With My Daughter —

My daughter was very close with her mom at the time. I had a lot of access [but] at the time, I was working more and I pretty much turned into my dad as far as [not being involved with my kids].

[I mean] we did things together on camping trips and whatnot. But the day to day life was more of just—we were in the same house, but there weren't a lot of deep conversations or closeness in that regard, with her and I during that period.

In a sense it was almost awkward. I'd push through that deliberately and spend time with my daughter, but I don't recall feeling really comfortable. It was more of, 'I know this is the right thing to do and so I need to do it even though I don't feel totally competent at how to relate to this young lady as she's growing up.'

I was still pulling out of my own hole. I think I had my own crap to deal with, so [even though] I had feelings about [what she was going through in her life], I didn't have the energy to process it with her.

— Early On Communication Was More By Osmosis Than Actual Conversation —

[So] most of the time, in the process of life, things were kind of dispersed by osmosis to [my kids] as far as my values and things. We didn't talk about it a lot. Whenever we had discussions about matters of consequence, I would dictate.

I mean, that's kind of a harsh word for it, but I would be the one who would say, 'This is how we do things and these are the rules,' and that kind of thing. Not in an overbearing way but just because I was the dad.

As far as discussions about how you deal with a moral choice, I would {basically be the one} talking about it. {Of course} there would be a little bit of back-and-forth.

– Things Are Finally Better—My Daughter Has Seen Me Work Past My Problems –

Now it's different. She's getting married {in a few weeks},

And I'm in a much better place myself, through a lot of hard work. So our conversations are definitely adult-to-adult. They're about, what I refer to as matters of consequence—values, what's going on in the world and how she feels about this and that.

Our conversations are more comfortable, they're easy. They're not as awkward, but largely that's because I have energy to do that. She's watched as I've worked through it.

She knew that, 'Gosh, Dad goes to counseling appointments and therapy.' She was aware of my work and she's very—I guess if I asked her, she'd probably say, 'Yeah, I'm proud of you for working through it dad.'

I had some really good therapy and I have a very good {men's} group that I hang out with on a weekly basis. It's just a really good maintenance program for that. {Also} got some pharmaceutical stuff dealing with the depression.

{So I guess} it was just a culmination of, I finally got ahead of it. But it was a lot of hard work.

Through the culmination of therapy, through my faith, through the group of guys that I meet with on a weekly basis, I'm just continually chipping away at it. I've finally got enough tools to stay ahead of it. I'd put it that way."

Richard, fifty year old male nurse anesthesiologist, father of a twenty-five year old daughter and two sons

A Great Dad Stays Involved With His Daughter Even After A Divorce

"[What does a daughter want from her dad]? A safe place, a guiding voice, encouragement without judgment, and of course love.

You know, in the case of my stepdaughter Tiffany, I've grown really close to her and she's grown really close to me.

[But] her biological father on the other hand is always trying to judge her. And he really doesn't spend much time with her.

He lived [nearby] in Colorado for about three years, but he hardly ever saw her, and that really made me sad. He would come and pick her up on the big holidays, Thanksgiving and Christmas, and take her to dinner or ask her over for dinner.

But for [the rest] of the time he wasn't a part of her life. I mean, he didn't go to her soccer games and other events, and didn't call her up to spend time with her. That made me sad for her."

Terry, sixty-two year old engineer and father of two sons age thirty-eight and thirty-four, a stepson age twenty-four and a twenty-one year old stepdaughter

A Daughter's Relationship With Mom Is Different Than With Dad

My Daughter Gets Something Different from Me Than From Her Mom

"I think my daughter wants more the love from her mom. I think I give her something different that she doesn't necessarily get from her mom—a sense of safety."

Ron, forty-seven year old school counselor and father of an eleven-year-old daughter and a twin eight-year-old daughter and son

Sometimes Your Daughter Will Want Her Mommy—Don't Take it Personally

"Understand that as your daughter grows up, for a lot of things she's going to look towards her mother. Don't take it personally, because that's just the nature of the human psyche.

There *will* be times and things that *you* and your daughter will have that your wife and she will not.

A child's relationship with mom and with dad is different.

Yet many dads experience a subtle jealousy or sadness that a mom may have a closer relationship than the dad.

It's going to be a relationship that changes, sometimes minute-by-minute, day-by-day, year-by-year. [Even when she's little] there will be times where it feels like she doesn't want to have anything to do with you, and then she turns right around and comes and crawls in bed with you. Those are the types of things that'll absolutely blow your mind."

Rob, forty-eight year old truck driver going to night school for massage therapy, father of a ten year old daughter and a twenty-three year old son (from a previous marriage who he also remains involved with)

I Struggled To Find The Time I Needed To Be A Good Father

Having Kids Was More Time-Consuming Than I Expected

> "I never knew how hard it would be to have kids. I really struggle with that one. Man they're time consuming {he nervously laughs}. It really surprised me."

> *Ron, forty-seven year old school counselor and father of an eleven-year-old daughter and a twin eight-year-old daughter and son*

Working and Going To School Leave Me Too Exhausted For My Family

> "I drive a truck during the day {so} I'm home every night. {But I also} go to school two nights a week, {and that's} time my son needs, time my wife needs, and time my daughter needs.

> {So} I have to kind of sit down and plan it out, seven days or so in advance.

> {Therefore} trying to be consistent both emotionally and, uh...

> Because of what I've been doing, I feel exhaustion. It plays a major part of the inconsistencies temperament-wise and attitude-wise in my interaction {with my family}."

> *Rob, forty-eight year old truck driver going to night school for massage therapy, father of a ten year old daughter and a twenty-three year old son (from a previous marriage who he also remains involved with)*

Being a Dad—I Miss The Things I've Had To Give Up

> "Yeah, I like being a dad {but} I miss my own time. I miss the things I've given up. I think that's the biggest challenge for me.

> Some dads are all about being a dad, and throwing themselves in it. They love it and they eat it up. They express these feelings that I just don't connect with.

I'm sad that I don't [feel the same way]. I want to, but I'm not a natural at this.

I've had people tell me what a great dad I am. But I'd be so much better if I could just willingly give up the things that I value so much in my life, things that I just love and adore, that are so important to me.

I'm trying to do it all. That gets in the way of me being as good a dad as I could be."

Ron, forty-seven year old father of an eleven-year-old daughter and a twin eight-year-old daughter and son

Being A Divorced Dad Was Tough At Times

The Worst Of The Worst Became Some Of The Best Times With My Kids

"[Being a single parent has been] very exhausting, overwhelming. It forced me to go dig very deep, and just find some way to get from one day to the next.

And yet in that context, at the worst-of-the-worst was when I had the best time with the kids. I think we remember that time as very special. [I mean], she's a tremendous daughter, she's a great daughter. Her cards, her special birthday cards. I know I'm in her heart all the time.

> Most dads gasped at the thought of being a *single* parent, having to raise a child on their own.
>
> Perhaps in part, that's why even those who had gone through a painful divorce stayed involved as a parent.

I'd hate to even think about [her not being part of my life]. Oh, God. I would not be as patient or sensitive or appreciative of women, or understanding of women or girls. I learned a lot. I would be much lonelier. I would feel like I missed a huge part of life."

Eric, fifty-two year old psychologist, father of a twenty-four year old daughter and a nineteen year old son (divorced when his daughter was six but stayed involved as a dad)

Only Seeing Her Every Other Weekend Is Hard

"Not having her live under my roof, seeing her every other weekend {because of the divorce}, having to continually say goodbye to her and not see her for two weeks at a time, has been sort of practice in {eventually} letting go of her {when she gets older}. It's still the hardest thing."

John, fifty-six year old schoolteacher, divorced father of eighteen year old daughter (divorced when his daughter was seven but remained close to her)

The Divorce Definitely Limited My Time With My Kids

"Post-divorce? Yeah, it sucked. It was terrible. {It'd be} just week-on, week-off and I wouldn't see my daughter that much during the week off.

I wasn't flying {as a commercial pilot} at that time {so I had more time to be with her}. {As a pilot}, being away at work in a hotel room and not having my kids, I am used to that. {But} being home and not having my kids is _not_ something I'm used to. So that was hard, yeah. It was hard to be at home and not really allowed to see my kids when they were right there.

Things are a lot better now. When I'm home and not working, I've got my kids full time. If I want to go see my daughter some afternoon, I can go see her. It's no problem.

But the divorce was definitely not harmonious."

Mark, forty-four year old Navy pilot, father of a fifteen year old daughter and an eleven year old son (divorced when his daughter was seven but stayed involved as a dad)

I Really Enjoy Being A Stepfather

Once You Get Past The Trust Thing It Can Be Really Fantastic

"It almost seems like being a stepdad is doing it with one hand tied behind your back at times. Yeah. You start out at a disadvantage.

But by the same token, that doesn't mean it can't be fantastic. In one sense it may [actually] have been helpful, being the stepdad in our particular situation, just because her father is, you know, very different from me.

[Her father] was very controlling so I think she had a void or a need in her life that I was able to step in and fill.

But we kind-of had to do this dance initially to where we could develop a trust relationship with each other. Then once we started to get past that, things just fell into place and worked really well, and continue to work really well."

Terry, sixty-two year old engineer and father of two sons age thirty-eight and thirty-four, a stepson age twenty-four and a twenty-one year old stepdaughter

Although They Have Similarities—Every Child Is Different

Each Of My Kids Is Different

"I mean, none of my three kids are alike. Doesn't mean they don't have some similarities but they're not the same kids."

Ron, forty-seven year old school counselor and father of an eleven-year-old daughter and a twin eight-year-old daughter and son

One Daughter Is Easier To Talk To Than The Other

It's Easier Having Meaningful Talks With One Of My Daughters

"Athena and I've been having deep meaningful conversations ever since she was a kid. When I moved [away] to San Diego

I would talk to Athena every day [on the phone], but [my other daughter] Danielle would be a blue moon. By 'blue moon' I mean maybe once-a-month I would be fortunate enough to talk to Danielle."

Aaron, thirty-two year old construction worker and ex-bouncer, father of two daughters age nine and ten (marriage fell apart after just a few years, but he has remained close to his daughters)

One Daughter Lets Me Know What She Wants—That Makes It Easier

"Maria in personality is more like me than her mother. She's very optimistic. She has an intrinsic sense of worth.

Because Maria and I are more sympathetic to nature, we'll go and hang out in the hammock even though there are mosquitoes. Or Maria will go camping with me out at the beach. [My older daughter] Natalia doesn't want to go camping because she's worried about the bugs and the hassles of camping, so to speak. In that way I interact differently [with each of them].

Dads often explained how different their relationship has been with one daughter compared to another.

One will be cheerful and tell you exactly how she's feeling, and that makes interaction with her easy.

The other will keep you guessing and insecure.

Maria, with great pride will say that she has pooped in the woods. Natalia would always say, 'Oh my God. I can't do that, oh terrible.' Maria says, 'It's just that, it's just dirt, it's just whatever.'

[As a family] we have done some pretty memorable trips. We have gone whale diving, with humpback whales. We've done dolphins. Natalia is not as enthusiastic about animal life and what-not [as Maria], but she likes the richness of having gone somewhere and done something.

[When it comes to] the physical contact, the embracing, the kissing good night, the affirmations, I think my two daughters are pretty similar. [And] their confidence is pretty similar.

[But] Natalia is not always forthcoming about her emotional downsides. Often it's me going in and checking in with her and lightly probing around her heart, her psyche at the time.

[By contrast] Maria is very easy to [understand]. She says what she wants. Sometimes we joke—we call her the 'gimme' child, the 'gimme' girl. You know, 'I want that, I want this, I want this, I want that.'

So it's easy to take that cue and develop an experience around it. Natalia doesn't come out so forthright with identifying what she wants. [Although] now it's coming more, but in the past it was hard to create experiences around her. Maria, she's easier to be with [in that way].

[Of course, both daughters] are available to [discuss] deep meaningful topics. It's just whether they really want to go through the weight of the conversation.

[For example] Maria is able to identify her discomforts, her fears and the source of them to me. 'Papa, I'm afraid when you shout.' 'Papa, I know when you're frustrated over the math. I can feel it. Can we stop?' You know, those kinds of things. And that's deep in the fact that she identifies something quickly and presents it.

Maria is always asking me for help on homework, so I do a lot more homework with Maria. [But] with Natalia, except for help with writing [when she was younger], she never comes to me with homework."

Andrew, forty-six year old schoolteacher, father of two daughters age nine and ten

I Had Fear And Resentment At Being Such A Young Father

I Resented That Her Becoming Pregnant Forced My Life To Change Direction

"I had a lot of anger towards myself and a lot of fear at having a child, [my] being twenty one at the time I got [my girlfriend] pregnant.

I had a lot of things going for me. I was looking into transferring to UC Berkley or UC Santa Cruz to play [college] rugby there. I walked away from that due to the fact of my actions.

My brother suggested I have an abortion, [but] I just didn't have it in me to do that. So we both decided to continue on and have the baby.

[But] my girlfriend at the time didn't feel like moving from the LA area away from her family to the Bay Area, so I didn't take on the, uh—I wouldn't say it would be a scholarship but they were definitely going to help me with getting into school.

So there was a lot of fear, a lot of resentment on her not really being too willing to go—and a lot of anger with myself. I should have just been more of a man in my decision making."

Aaron, thirty-two year old construction worker and ex-bouncer, father of two daughters age nine and ten (marriage fell apart after just a few years, but he has remained close to his daughters)

Being A Father Is The Most Incredible Thing In My Life

For Me, Being A Father Is Absolutely Incredible

"I knew I wanted to be a dad, but I never realized how absolutely, incredibly fun it was, and how incredibly proud I would be of my daughter.

I always felt that I would be proud of her because she was my daughter. I never realized that I would be proud of her because she is this incredible human being.

The thing is, being a dad for me has been a fulfillment of a huge long, long dream. But what I love most is that it just keeps growing. As the years expand, it's like, 'Oh wow!' I don't even remember dreaming that [it would be like this]. So the dream just keeps expanding.

I'm just so incredibly proud of my daughter as a human being and I am proud to tell that to everybody I know."

Lucas, fifty year old kindergarten teacher, father of a twenty-five year old daughter (divorced when his daughter was four but stayed one-hundred percent involved throughout her entire life)

My Kids Are My Fan Club—There's Something Pretty Wonderful About That

"I did a triathlon and [my kids] were all very supportive of me. They always make a big deal of it.

It's nice to have a fan club in some way. I've got a real fan club, you know. My own children are truly part of my fan club.

This concept of your kids being your fan club is interesting.

Even dads with challenging relationships with a daughter often described this feeling of being unconditionally loved.

34

If you [don't have] kids, I'm not sure who your fan club is. There's something pretty neat about having people that truly care about you. It makes you internally feel wonderful."

Len, sixty-eight year old attorney, father of a thirty-five year old son, a thirty-four year old daughter and a twenty-eight year old stepdaughter

A Life Without Kids Is Half-A-Life—But Some Guys Are Not Meant To Be Dads

"A life not lived being a parent is half a life.

I tell that to my buddy who didn't have kids. I says, 'You're living a selfish half-a-life. You can't expect to have fully lived at the end of your days without having gone through this process of making a new generation, of making a new branch on a tree.'

Yeah, I even bought him a copy of *Chicken Soup for the Father's Soul* and gave it to him, but I don't think it moved him very much.

[I think,] 'If this book didn't move you then maybe you shouldn't be a dad. Maybe everybody's not made to be a dad. Maybe you are just too selfish to be a dad."

Ken, 9/11 New York City fireman and father of a six year old daughter and two sons

Without My Daughter My Life Would Be Flat—She's Brought Me So Much Joy

'[If I never had my daughter]… now that's sad. My life would be empty. It would be like a book with half the pages ripped out. I mean, like all the pages are there, but—so one-hundred-fifty pages in the book, there's still one-hundred-fifty pages but each page is ripped vertically in half. It's just missing [a part]. That's what it would be like.

[I'd be] missing a lot of joy. She's brought so much joy into my life.

Not having my daughter Savannah in my life, it would just spin. It would be a bit less full and just flat. Just a lot of emptiness. That's it."

Mark, forty-four year old Navy pilot, father of a fifteen year old daughter and an eleven year old son (divorced when his daughter was seven but stayed involved as a dad)

Some Surprises from this Chapter

On Being the Father of a Daughter

- **Fear of Women:** One surprise was the dads who used the word "fear" when describing interactions with their daughter – a sense of walking on eggshells.

  For some it was an extension of their fear around women in general ("I don't really understand the rules of engagement as I do with men") while others described it as an uneasiness over a daughter's unpredictable moodiness ("She gets mad and I don't always know why").

- **How Dad's Parents Affected Him:** As we'd expect, many dads mirrored their own father in being emotionally distant. The surprise came from how many of these dads suffered as a result, explaining their longing for a better relationship with their daughter but just not knowing how.

  It was encouraging that a few of these dads pushed past their discomfort and actually took steps to interact, periodically taking a daughter out for dinner, for example.

  It was also encouraging that several dads who had suffered physical or emotional abuse or rejection from their own father (or mother) swore they would break the cycle *("I'll never be like him – my daughter will never have to experience anything like that!")*. Of course, some dads were more effective than others at overcoming these types of emotional bruises.

Stage One: Newborn

— First Contact —

Defining Factor: A totally helpless child comes into the world.

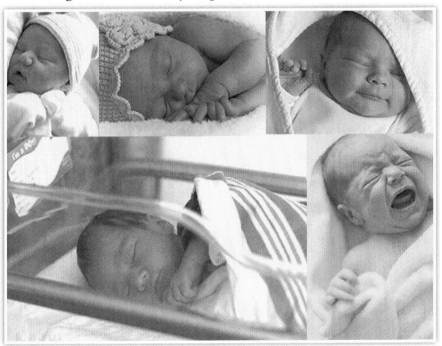

From realizing HIS child
is about to be born
to holding her in his arms
for the first time
this chapter walks you through
the feelings of
confusion and self-doubt
for many dads
to the indescribable moment
where he holds his daughter
for the first time
to the emotional upheaval
in the days and months
following the birth.

Not every father
will be applauded
but the struggles and extraordinary
triumphs of character
will open the eyes
of many who
read this chapter.

Inside this Chapter

Observations from 101 Dads of Daughters

- You Gotta Be There For The Birth Of Your Daughter
- Fathers Were Not Always Allowed In The Delivery Room
- Maybe It Was Easy For Some—But For Us Conceiving Was Difficult
- The Actual Delivery Was Very Exciting And Intense

- That Feeling Of Holding A Tiny Defenseless Child Was Amazing
- I Felt A Sudden Fear About Becoming A Father
- Naming My Daughter Was A Pretty Important Moment

You Gotta Be There For The Birth Of Your Daughter

At That Moment When Your Child is Born—You Gotta Be There!

"How do you miss the start of your child's life? It was terrific. Oh yeah, absolutely. I can't imagine missing that. That's the most important day of her life.

To take care of this helpless life that's going to rely on you for quite a few years, to make all of the decisions and do all of the providing for her. You gotta be there at that moment.

Plus it's probably the most stressful and dramatic event of a woman's life and she shouldn't be there alone."

Ken, 9/11 New York City fireman and father of a six year old daughter and two sons

Fathers Were Not Always Allowed In The Delivery Room

They Kept Fathers In The Waiting Room

"I was on the other side of the lake. Back in those days [having a father present in the delivery] was not part of the whole thing. They had to wait in the waiting room."

Carl, sixty-five year old ex-music teacher, with forty, thirty-eight and thirty-six year old daughters (divorced twenty years ago but stayed involved as their dad)

Maybe It Was Easy For Some—But For Us Conceiving Was Difficult

After A Miscarriage, The Next Child Was Very Special

"We had one child that we lost in a miscarriage and that was very painful. My feeling is the miscarriage was a boy. [So when we were pregnant about a year later with Natalia], my sense was it's going to be a girl and I was delighted by that."

Andrew, forty-six year old schoolteacher, father of two daughters age nine and ten

It's Incredibly Painful Watching Your Friends Get Pregnant When You Can't

"We spent years trying to get pregnant.

Did you ever see the movie Forget Paris? Great movie. They talk about this whole thing—where the couple is trying to get pregnant, and how difficult it was, and the anguish and pain that's tied up in it. They totally nailed it. I mean, whoever wrote it really must have gone through it.

It's an incredibly painful period of our lives, to be trying to get pregnant and she can't get pregnant. Being around all your friends who are getting pregnant, and then having their kids, and wondering if you'll ever have kids. Maybe you never will. To be there for your friends, for their joy, [when you] are struggling to do that, [boy that's tough]."

Ron, forty-seven year old school counselor and father of an eleven-year-old daughter, a twin eight-year-old daughter and son

Finally Being In The Delivery Room After Three Years Of Trying—It Was Amazing!

"It took us three years to have Elizabeth. We finally had Elizabeth using fertility treatments. We had one round of—not in-vitro fertilization, [it was] intro-uterine fertilization–so it was like they took my sperm and put it into her uterus at a time when she was ovulating, and the two met.

[My wife] Julie thinks she was pregnant before they actually did the insertion. But anyway, we have a wonderful child. [And finally being in the delivery room] was totally amazing."

Andy, forty-six year old TV reporter, father of a nine year old daughter (recently divorced but remains close to his daughter)

The Actual Delivery Was Very Exciting And Intense

The Delivery Was More Intense Than What They Show In The Movies

"[Being in the delivery room was] fun, exhilarating, and scary as hell at the end.

I also liked being there to support my wife and help her get through it. I'd never seen anyone [get] an epidural before, so that was interesting.

When my daughter was born, I didn't know what a newborn looks like when they first come out because, the way the movies and TV shows portray this, is not real.

A newborn that comes out, they have a purple hue to their skin color until they pink up. And they have that white film [around them] to help them come out easier.

When they come out in most of the TV [shows] and movies I have seen, they come out so clean that they don't need to be cleaned— and understandably. I mean, how you gonna fake it if you're using an actual baby.

[After they delivered her] I walked over there to stay with my daughter as they cleaned her up. I didn't want to be far from her.

Then... I looked over and saw them vigorously working on my wife. [I saw] blood spurting out from my wife because the placenta ruptured a bloodline inside, and I went from being an excited new father to thinking I was about to be a single dad who's gonna bury my wife.

I also had no idea about the after-birth. I didn't even know what it was, didn't know it existed. So that was a freaky experience too. It was like, 'What are they doing? What's that coming out of her? Oh my god!' {he laughs} So that was bizarre too.

Fortunately my wife was okay. She was incredibly groggy for a long time because she lost a ton of blood, [but she was fine].

So yeah. I'll never forget that [experience]. I have a vivid memory of it."

Ron, forty-seven year old school counselor and father of an eleven-year-old daughter, a twin eight-year-old daughter and son

That Feeling Of Holding A Tiny Defenseless Child Was Amazing

My Daughter Was Premature—I Was Going To Do Whatever It Took To Save Her

"When I saw she was no larger than the size of my hand, and she was laid out under a heat lamp or a warming lamp, and they were trying to get needles in her, I knew what was coming {he struggles through his tears}.

My purpose was to find a way for this child to live. So I went back home and I flooded several websites with questions—what can I do; what's happening; here's the child, here's the circumstances."

Andrew, forty-six year old schoolteacher, father of two daughters age nine and ten

From That First Moment—I Fell In Total Love With My Daughter

"I remember there was a lot of blood on the floor and stuff like that. And I have difficulties with blood, so I was sitting in the corner trying not to faint into the operating theater.

But when she came out after twenty-six hours of labor and an emergency C-section, I remember I thought she was absolutely gorgeous, beautiful. [I] fell in love, total love, permanently. And I was involved with her heavy duty from the first minute."

Eric, fifty-two year old psychologist, father of a twenty-four year old daughter and a nineteen year old son (divorced when his daughter was six but stayed involved as a dad)

I Loved My Freedom—But Something Changed When I First Held My Daughter

"First of all, I never thought I would have a kid. I just never did. Actually, I never thought I would be married either.

It's not like I was some big player out there or anything like that. It's just that, I guess I was kind of a free-lancer. I really appreciated my freedom. If I needed to cut and run, I could do that.

By far, the majority of dads told us how something unexpected happened once they held that tiny defenseless life in their hands for the first time.

Some dads who did not intend to stick around, could not explain why suddenly they could not leave.

[But when I first held my daughter}... I mean, my kid in my arms. I held her. I cut the umbilical cord. There's nothing like that. There was never an event in my life that was ever like that at all."

Ray, forty-eight year old computer executive, father of a five year old daughter

Holding A Tiny Defenseless Child In Your Arms—It Was Amazing

"[If you miss the delivery] what you will miss of course is holding that child when it is so tiny and so defenseless. You are [suddenly] so important because that child won't survive without you. [If you miss the delivery] you'll miss that part."

George, seventy-five year old father of fifty-two year old daughter and two sons; also later became stepfather of another daughter (when she was a teenager) and a stepson

Something Inside Me Changed The Moment I Held That Tiny Baby In My Arms

> "I remember the very moment that I saw [my new daughter] Karla in the labor room, and I took her in my arms. That very moment I was changed. Something inside of me was changed that I cannot explain. In that very moment, I felt the 'spirits' to be the father.
>
> That was the same thing exactly that happened when my parents died. When my father and my mother [were gone], I felt that a point of reference was lost. And when I held Karla in my arms, in my hands, that very day I felt something different. I said, 'I am a father. She's my daughter.' "

> *Jose, fifty-four year old therapist and television personality, father of a twenty-eight year old daughter (divorced, and recently reconnected with his daughter after a ten-year absence—he is humbled that she has forgiven him)*

I Felt a Sudden Fear About Becoming A Father

I Was Scared About What Kind of Father I Would Be

> "I think I was really scared during the entire pregnancy about what fatherhood was going to be like and what kind of a father I would be.
>
> But as soon as I saw my baby come out, I was just blown wide open emotionally. I was blown wide open in terms of my fathering instincts, in terms of my instinct to protect this child no matter what. And I just was in love and adored her from the moment I saw her."

> *Andy, forty-six year old TV reporter, father of a nine year old daughter (recently divorced but remains close to his daughter)*

I Suddenly Realized That I Had To Care For Someone Other Than Myself

> "[Her birth] was a joy but it was also a dawning of a tremendous amount of responsibility. The realization that I had to start caring for someone other than myself."

Arthur, fifty-nine year old father of eight kids, including six daughters ranging from age fourteen to thirty-two

I Was Elated And Worried At The Same Time

"Emotionally, I had pretty much come to the fact that, 'Okay, this child's being born. I want to be part of its life.'

Emotionally, it was a very great day. I was walking on cloud nine when she was born. But still [there's] the fear of, 'Am I going to be able to take care of them, take care of the two of them [my wife and my daughter], and how is [my daughter] going to turn out?'

You know, the typical parent reaction. Mixed emotions, I guess is the best way to put it. Both elated and worried at the same time."

Rob, forty-eight year old truck driver going to night school for massage therapy, father of a ten year old daughter and a twenty-three year old son (from a previous marriage who he also remains involved with)

Naming My Daughter Was A Pretty Important Moment

I Wanted My Daughter To Have A Name That Was Meaningful And Distinctive

"For the longest time my wife and I said if we ever had a daughter we were going to name her Ashley Nicole, and we were set.

[But then], like four months before my daughter was born I [realized that] I wanted her to have a name that was just her own and distinctive, and there was something about Ashley Nicole that just didn't fit right with me.

[So my wife said], 'Then come to me with a list of names and I'll look at them.'

I did all of my research, and then I said, 'Iman is the name that I like. Iman means faith.'

She said okay, and so that's what it is {he laughs}."

Darryl, forty-seven year old business executive, father of a seventeen year old son and a fourteen year old daughter

I Didn't Get To Choose The Name That I Really Wanted For My Daughter

"I was going to name my daughter Athena Celestine because I thought 'heavenly wisdom' would be beautiful. Unfortunately my ex wife thought that sounded like the name of a pizza—that all the kids would beat up on her and make fun of her. So I had to sacrifice once again something. She decided to name her Erin Athena. [At least] we agreed to call her Athena by her middle name."

Aaron, thirty-two year old construction worker and ex-bouncer, father of two daughters age nine and ten (marriage fell apart after just a few years, but he has remained close to his daughters)

Some Surprises from this Chapter

On Being the Father of a Daughter

- **The Magic of Holding a Defenseless Infant:** It was surprising that even the few dads who considered abandoning their new family early on, were somehow transformed once they held their newborn daughter for the first time.

  There was something in the tactile experience of holding a helpless infant that seemed to trigger a deep-rooted parenting instinct in most of these dads.

- **Fear of Fatherhood:** This tactile experience of holding a helpless infant also aroused a momentary fear in many that they might not be a good dad.

  It was fascinating that cradling a helpless baby in his arms would awaken so much for so many of new dads.

Stage Two: Age 0-2 – Awareness

– The Good, the Bad and the Cuddly –

Defining Factors: She becomes aware of her mother (the first woman in her life), her father (the first man in her life), and siblings if any. She learns to speak her first words, take her first steps, and regulate bodily functions.

She also learns how she fits into the family – whether she is loved, ignored or a burden. Girls tend to concentrate on facial expressions, emotions and speech more than boys.

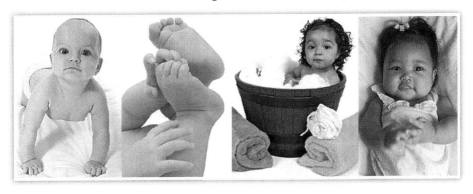

In these early months
a father's
personal and social life
are overtaken
by this
tiny needy "alien."

In this chapter
we observe the
time challenges and guilt
on one side
and the incredible highs
that come from
hugging and playing
with this
interactively curious
little person.

Inside this Chapter

Observations from 101 Dads of Daughters

- Early On I Didn't Have Much Time For My Daughter
- My Job Allowed Me Plenty Of Time To Spend With My Daughter
- I Loved Holding Her And Having Her Fall Asleep On Me

- There Were Tough Moments—And Really Great Ones
- My Daughter Had Some Health Issues When She Was Young
- In The Beginning I Didn't Deal With Being A Dad Very Well
- Wow—Having Twins Plus Another Child Is Quite A Challenge

Early On I Didn't Have Much Time For My Daughter

As A New Doctor With A Failing Marriage—I Missed Much Of Her Childhood

> "I was busy enough in the first couple of years of family practice and emergency medicine that I don't remember [time with my daughter] as well as I wish I did.
>
> And to some extent, my memories are impacted by the fact that [my] relationship with her mom was coming apart."
>
> *Carl, fifty-nine year old M.D. and director of an international non-profit organization, father of a twenty-one year old daughter (divorced when his daughter was four but stayed involved as a dad)*

Between My Job And The Divorce—I Didn't Spend Much Time With My Daughter

> "I got out of the Navy and I flew in the airlines for about three and a half years. [But that kept me away from my family, so] I left that and was working for about a year and a half in business. You know, working in business development, in technology, a company with a guy I knew. So I was home every day, although I was working a lot and also doing some traveling. [But in general] I was home.
>
> Then that fell apart so I was going to try and get a job back with the airlines. And I went through the divorce so I wasn't with my daughter every day because she was half with her mother and half with me."
>
> *Mark, forty-four year old Navy pilot, father of a fifteen year old daughter and an eleven year old son (divorced when his daughter was seven but stayed involved as a dad)*

I Didn't Spend Much Time With My Kids—I Was Too Busy Trying To Feed Them

> "I don't remember too much about the kids because I was rarely around except when there was a fight or something. I was not

too close with none of them as a matter of fact, because I was never there. I was out trying to feed [them]."

Walter, eighty-one year old retired businessman, father of a fifty-six year old daughter and three sons

Coming Back From War—I Was A Stranger To My Daughter—That Was Really Hard

"Elizabeth was born on Thanksgiving Day. I was in Korea at the time, in the army.

When Liz was born, she and her mom and sister were living with my wife's parents [for] about 6 months. My wife was trying very hard to get me out through the Red Cross. She contacted [President] Jerry Ford who happened to be our [state] representative, and within about three days I was on a plane flying home.

The strange thing for me was, when I saw Liz, she did not want to come to me. She was like six months old and she was afraid of anybody but her mom—and that was hard, that was hard to deal with.

It took almost, I'd say seven months to really get her to feel like she was comfortable sitting on my lap and reacting with me and all that kind of stuff. Yeah, it was a difficult time."

Carl, sixty-five year old ex-music teacher, with forty, thirty-eight and thirty-six year old daughters (divorced twenty years ago but stayed involved as their dad)

Between My Job And Night School—I Don't Have Much Energy For My Family

"There were times I was [emotionally] distant because I was so exhausted. I couldn't keep my eyes open.

[When my daughter was] about three or four, I started driving for a trucking company, so I was on the road during the week and came home on the weekends. I had one day that I'd just do nothing but darn near sleep. Then [otherwise] it was just family time. I'd spend as much time with them as possible.

[But] I would have to say, for about five or six years I was just so physically [and] emotionally exhausted at the same time, I didn't have a whole lot to give. That precipitated a change in jobs, because I wanted to be more a part of my daughter's life than I had been previously in my son's life. I'm still working to that end to be more a part of her life. That's a daily struggle.

[Now] I drive a truck during the day and I'm home every night. [But I'm also] going to school two nights a week—time my son needs, and time my wife needs, and time my daughter needs. So I have to kind of, sit down and plan out [my time with them] a week or so in advance."

Rob, forty-eight year old truck driver going to night school for massage therapy, father of a ten year old daughter and a twenty-three year old son (from a previous marriage who he also remains involved with)

My Job Allowed Me Plenty Of Time To Spend With My Daughter

My Job Finally Gave Me More Time To Spend With My Kids

"When [my daughter] Iman was born, [my wife] had just finished with her MBA so she was home with Iman. I was not traveling as much, so I actually got to spend a lot of time with her when she was very young. I was home every night pretty much her first two years. So we were in heavy kid-mode.

> For those dads who had the time or took the time, this seemed to be an important bonding period with their new daughter.
>
> Many who could not find the time or energy because of career or school expressed guilt at missing this early period with their daughter.

58

[My son] was very young, and he was not quite potty trained yet. [Actually] he forgot his potty training when his sister was born, I do recall that. So it was exciting times to have two in diapers at the same time."

Darryl, forty-seven year old business executive, father of a seventeen year old son and a fourteen year old daughter

Working Out Of My Home Meant I Could Be With My Daughter Big-Time

"Yeah, [when my daughter was young I was able to be with her] big-time because I worked out of my house, so I was here all the time."

Ed, fifty-one year old realtor, father of a fifteen year old daughter and two sons (divorced when his daughter was older to reduce the trauma he and his wife experienced, both being children of divorce)

Shift Work Allowed Me To Spend A Lot Of Time With My Daughter

"It was great. Because of the shift work, you're home a lot. You get to spend a lot of time at home.

[As a firefighter] we work twenty-four hours at a time, so you have days off in between. Most people work forty hours a week. We work forty-eight hours a week. Still, it's only two twenty-four-hour [shifts] a week, so you have a lot of time to be dad.

I was fortunate enough to have spent a lot of time with my daughter. Her toddler years I was her main care giver. My wife was at work and I was at home with her.

I would lay on the floor with her and play with her and read with her. I bathed her and fed her and changed the diapers."

Ken, 9/11 New York City fireman and father of a six year old daughter and two sons

I Loved Holding Her And Having Her Fall Asleep On Me

I'd Cradle Her In My Lap And Make Faces

> "I loved holding her. I loved curling her up in my lap with my knees up by a coffee table, and letting her cradle in there, and making faces at her."
>
> *Craig, thirty-nine year old father of a ten year old son, eight year old daughter and fifteen month old son*

When My Daughter Was An Infant—I Loved Her Falling Asleep On My Chest

> "I just remember the standard baby stuff. Really nothing unique. Crying a lot, sleeping a lot, up at all hours until she developed a routine. When we were first trying to feed her food, spitting it up all the time. I remember the burps.
>
> But what I fondly remember is her falling asleep on me. I used to love her falling asleep on me.
>
> I actually had no problem getting her in the middle of the night when I felt like she would fall back asleep soon. I loved to fall asleep with her asleep on my chest.
>
> I would get on the couch and put pillows on the side of me so she wouldn't roll off me when I fell asleep too. I'd get her to fall asleep on me rather than put her back in her crib and run the risk of her waking up again [when I moved her].
>
> So I would sit or lie down on the couch and fall asleep with her. That's where my wife would find us. That was great."
>
> *Ron, forty-seven year old school counselor and father of an eleven-year-old daughter and a twin eight-year-old daughter and son*

My Daughter Climbed Out Of Her Crib So She Could Sleep With Us

"[My daughter] was my shadow, she was my twin. She always wanted to be with me.

She'd sleep with her arm underneath my back, just for warmth I believe, and [for] connection. [Back then] we lived in a place that wasn't the best during winters so we would all sleep together.

I didn't know [if that was] right or wrong. But I remember just one time we put her in the crib. She was just so accustomed to sleeping with us or being near me and her mother. But I remember one night Athena was crying and crying and screaming cause she didn't want to be in there. So she ended up jumping off the crib and somehow getting out, and running in bed with us. [It was then that I realized] she has a definite fire about her. She knows what she wants.

I [also] had a stepson that would sleep on [our] bed too, so go figure."

Aaron, thirty-two year old construction worker and ex-bouncer, father of two daughters age nine and ten (marriage fell apart after just a few years, but he has remained close to his daughters)

My Daughter Was Rambunctious And Cuddly

"[As a young child my daughter] was very rambunctious. She could be a little bit of a terror at times. But she could also be very sweet and cuddly."

Ed, fifty-one year old realtor, father of a fifteen year old daughter and two sons (divorced when his daughter was older to reduce the trauma he and his wife experienced, both being children of divorce)

The Miracle Of Creating This Child Brought Me Back To Church

"I found myself on our bed with [my new daughter] on my belly, just awestruck at what [my wife] and I had created. The miracle of her existence.

It actually brought me back to the church because [up until that time] I was my typical doubter atheist from college. [As a] philosophy major I learned there are other things besides religion.

But the miracle of her birth actually took me back to church."

George, seventy-five year old father of fifty-two year old daughter and two sons; also later became stepfather of another daughter (when she was a teenager) and a stepson

There Were Tough Moments—But Then There Were The Really Great Ones

Her Waking Up Every Two Hours Was Tough—But She Was So Much Fun And Giggly!

"I remember her as a lot of fun—playful, giggly. You could throw her around, she thought that was hilarious. Every bath was fun. Everything was fun.

I mean, she'd wake up every two hours to feed, so she was tough in that sense. But I remember her as a lot of fun."

Eric, fifty-two year old psychologist, father of a twenty-four year old daughter and a nineteen year old son (divorced when his daughter was six but stayed involved as a dad)

My Daughter Was Independent—She Didn't Always Want to Be Held

"I would have to say she was *not* really needy.

She was vocal but not crying all the time. She interacted very readily with people, [and was] a very quick learner. One day she pretty much decided to potty train herself. Intelligent. Inquisitive.

For some, these early years had hot-and-cold elements.

Periodic rejection hurt many dads deeply.

But the high moments seemed to more than compensate for the feeling of momentary emotional pain.

Sometimes she liked to be held and other times she didn't want anything to do with it. It all depended, I guess, on the way she was feeling or what she wanted to do."

Rob, forty-eight year old truck driver going to night school for massage therapy, father of a ten year old daughter and a twenty-three year old son (from a previous marriage who he also remains involved with)

Right Out of the Box She Was Artistic, Like Her Mom

"My strongest memory was my daughter was a beautiful sweet strong kid, loved to dance, and was pretty precocious with drawing and pictures and stuff. Right out of the box she seemed to be wired toward the same kind of artistic stuff that her mom had been."

Carl, fifty-nine year old M.D. and director of an international non-profit organization, father of a twenty-one year old daughter (divorced when his daughter was four but stayed involved as a dad)

My Daughter Always Had So Much Fun—It Was Great Doing Things With Her

"She's into the music and the dancing and the singing. She's just always had a lot of joy from all of that stuff. So as a real young child it was great being around her. She had a lot of youthful, playful energy. Couldn't wait to act out, always wanted to wear costumes. It was great—and it was great doing it with her."

Craig, thirty-nine year old father of a ten year old son, eight year old daughter and fifteen month old son

She Was a Fussy Baby But People Loved Being Around Her

"As a very young child my daughter was fussy. She wasn't colic or anything but she was hard to get to sleep.

When she was older, like a year old, she wasn't really good about playing by herself. She wasn't one of those kids that would just sit there and play. She needed to have somebody to play with.

[Physically] she was a real small baby. She was a very, very pretty girl, and smiled a lot. Everybody loves being around her, and they loved being around her as a little child too."

Mark, forty-four year old Navy pilot, father of a fifteen year old daughter and an eleven year old son (divorced when his daughter was seven but stayed involved as a dad)

She Was A Real Cutie When She Was Born

"With all our kids I really really appreciated watching my wife hold all of them. Just that image of the breastfeeding—this mother nurturing her children. It was unbelievable to me.

And this was our princess. I remember saying that, 'I now have a princess, a boy and a girl.' It was great. I was very excited it was a girl when she was born. She was a cutie. Oh, yeah, I loved holding her."

Craig, thirty-nine year old father of a ten year old son, eight year old daughter and fifteen month old son

She Had This Strange Funny Thing She Would Say

"{He laughs} Out-of-the-blue she came up with this word that she just liked to say, and that was 'Nat.' I have no idea where it came from.

'Nat, nat, nat, nat, nat, nat.' Like where is that from? 'Nat, nat, nat, nat, nat, nat.'

I have no idea to this day where that came from. I even got that on videotape at one point. I'll never be able to explain it and make any sense at all."

Ron, forty-seven year old school counselor and father of an eleven-year-old daughter and a twin eight-year-old daughter and son

My Daughter Likes Being Boss—Especially To Her Younger Sister

"The fact that she's the oldest really plays very well for her, because she loves to boss her siblings around.

She is at times really sweet and nice with them and plays with them and laughs and jokes with them. Other times, she can be pretty tough and mean to her younger sister.

I don't see her do that with her young brother, but she [and her brother] usually tag team against the younger sister."

Ron, forty-seven year old school counselor and father of an eleven-year-old daughter and a twin eight-year-old daughter and son

My Daughter Had Some Health Issues When She Was Young

My Daughter Cried A Lot When She Was Younger

"I remember her crying a lot. I think she might have had some ear trouble. We got her checked out [and they said she was fine] but she used to cry a lot so I don't know. I still kind of wonder what that was about."

Aaron, thirty-two year old construction worker and ex-bouncer, father of two daughters age nine and ten (marriage fell apart after just a few years, but he has remained close to his daughters)

She Had Ear Infections As A Young Child

"I remember her being a pretty sweet kid [but] with episodes of ear infections and pain and sleepless nights."

Carl, fifty-nine year old M.D. and director of an international non-profit organization, father of a twenty-one year old daughter (divorced when his daughter was four but stayed involved as a dad)

The effect of a daughter's early illness was dramatic for many dads.

Even older dads in their eighties could recall health issues their daughter had in her early years.

Even With Her Eye Half Shut, You Couldn't Help Falling Madly In Love With Her

"Oh man. Her first year she had this clogged tear duct, so she would be constantly getting some eye infections.

Here was this beautiful little creature with an eye half shut. You couldn't help but just be completely and madly in love with her, because [even with that eye shut] she would 'coo' and 'gaa' and make sounds, and really want to communicate with you."

Craig, thirty-nine year old father of a ten year old son, eight year old daughter and fifteen month old son

I Spent A Lot Of Time Rocking Her—It Helped Bond Us Later In Life

"Aimee, when she was a newborn, had colic. I spent a lot of time rocking her through the night, and comforting her because of her cramps in her stomach. I would hum to her. I would sing to her to try and calm her down. I think that did a lot for my bonding with my daughter early on."

Donnie, fifty-six year old father of a thirty-two year old daughter and thirty year old son (divorced when his daughter was eight but remained close to her)

My Son Had Colic, But My Daughter Was Very Easy

"Oh yeah. [My daughter was a] very easy, very happy child.

I remember my son was just the opposite. He had a very hard birth and early childhood. He had colic and everything. But my daughter was very easy, very contented, very happy all time."

Leonard, seventy-three year old ex- school music teacher, father of a forty-six year old son and a thirty-three year old daughter (divorced later in life but has stayed close to his daughter)

In The Beginning I Didn't Deal With Being A Dad Very Well

I Felt Suffocated But I Didn't Want My Daughter To Grow Up Without A Dad

"When we had our child, I think there were moments when I didn't display a whole lot of patience—with the whole crying all night and my wife being in total pain, and getting absolutely no sleep for days on end.

> Over and over again this theme would come up, that fatherhood was a learning process.
>
> The transition away from selfishness seemed to be an essential part of the journey.

I don't think I was doing that very well. I was pretty intolerant. Now when I think of that, I feel sadness. I feel, 'God, what a [jerk] I could be.'

[But during those early days] I felt suffocated, like I couldn't breathe. Over the course of four to six months I became severely depressed. Also, I was changing jobs and was under this economic stress. I thought my wife and I, our relationship was really just going down the tubes. I felt disconnected from her. I felt this totally emotional disconnection.

[I decided], 'I'm not doing anybody any good being here. Maybe I'm doing more harm than good.' So I felt like I had to separate.

We separated for five or six months. Of course, every day I went back to see my wife and see my child. It's not like I just fled the scene or anything like that.

[But eventually I realized] I didn't want my child to grow up without a dad.

I grew up for the most part without a dad—and when I did get a dad, it was an abusive-as-hell dad. He was an alcoholic and a rage-aholic and was physically abusive. I mean, seriously physically abusive. He was abusive to my mom too.

So I knew what I *didn't* want to be like.

I didn't want to be an absentee guy. I needed to do the right thing, to try and figure out how my wife and I could co-exist—and even more than that—to create a better relationship, but certainly co-exist and do the best thing for our daughter.

My wife and I are the kind of people who don't really tolerate mediocre anything. So if we're going to co-exist, we have to create a better relationship for ourselves. It was like an evolution.

– Men's Work Really Helped—It Gave Me Tools And Perspective –

Also, after doing [some really intense men's work], I learned how to completely flip my perspective and shift my consciousness, and open myself up to the fact that, wow, if I really tried, I could help make this whole situation work. That training really, really opened me up to the possibility that this could all work—and gave me tools to deal with it.

So I decided to really show up and be present after the training. I mean, it sounds real smarmy and commercialist but it's the truth.

[It also helped that my daughter] was beautiful. She had this spirit that was so radiant. She was—oh man, it's the tidal wave of love and joy and just beauty. Every day that I experienced her, I just wanted to breathe her into my soul. It's just so immense, the love. She was just pure love. She was pure love.

— I Love That My Daughter Could Understand What Was Really Happening —

Me and my wife, we decided to take [my daughter] when she was maybe a year and a half old, to Sedona Arizona with us. We were going to check out the vortexes and the energy fields there.

I had one of those little backpacks for kids, that you put them in so you can walk and have your hands free.

I remember her the whole time looking at the trees.

[Then my wife] steps on a rock and twists her ankle really bad. I mean, really bad. You could see it swell up and the whole bit.

So I pop up and say, 'You got to walk [it off] now. If that thing swells up, forget about it. You won't be able to walk on it. You gotta get up.'

She looks at me and she's like, 'Well that's not real tolerant.'

I said, 'Look, I'm not trying to be mean or rude. But if you don't get up and walk on it, you won't be able to. I can carry [our] kid. I'm pretty strong. But [I can't carry you as well].

[To help] I got her a little staff that she could put her weight on and walk.

But I remember my daughter the whole time. She was so receptive to everything that was going on. She'd display sadness and joy. When my wife started walking, [my daughter] just had this look of recognition and awareness about what was going on."

Ray, forty-eight year old computer executive, father of a five year old daughter

Wow—Having Twins Plus Another Child Is Quite A Challenge

Energy-Wise It's Tough Having Twins Plus Another Child

"It's a challenge, two babies in the house and a two-and-a-half-year-old.

Oh my God, time wise, energy wise, everything wise!

We're blessed that we lived in a city where our family is. When my oldest daughter was born, we were house-sitting across the street from my in-laws so my mother-in-law was {helping with} everything.

Now, we're gonna have a two-and-a-half year old *and* twins.

My mother-in-law moved in for a little while {so that really helped}. It's difficult with one, two is just unbelievably. I can't even imagine beyond two."

Ron, forty-seven year old school counselor and father of an eleven-year-old daughter and a twin eight-year-old daughter and son

Some Surprises from this Chapter

Dads with an Infant Daughter under Age Two

- **Time and Guilt:** Although some dads had plenty of time to spend with their daughters during these formative early years, most did not – with many voicing shame or regret at their seeming failure as a parent.

  Surprisingly, a few dads actually changed careers or restructured their lives so they could make time to be with their daughter, but these were the exceptions.

- **Fatherly Patience and Guilt:** Guilt seemed to be a common theme with many of the dads. And none more pronounced than the guilt many felt over not having had enough patience as a father.

  Crying babies suddenly taking over their life; having to give up their favorite pastimes to devote time to parenting.

  Some dads rolled with it. But many behaved badly as they grappled with this takeover of their personal life. These dads often voiced a sense of guilt even decades later that subtly impacted the relationship with their daughter, and their own sense of self-worth (*"I don't deserve her love because of how I acted"*).

- **That Little Heartbeat:** However, through all the complexity of being a new father, almost every dad mentioned how an infant daughter falling asleep on his chest or his lap was just magical.

  Again the tactile interaction with his daughter resonated for most dads. There was something about that little heartbeat, the rhythmic breathing and that tiny personality, that seemed to connect at a deep level with almost all these fathers.

Stage Three: Age 2 – Assertiveness

– The Terrible, Wonderful Twos –

Defining Factor: She learns to say NO. She realizes that she has the power to disagree. She wants her way, even if she doesn't know what her way is.

She is learning that she can assert herself, often not really knowing what she wants – simply knowing she wants something different from what you want.

Suddenly
his daughter has learned
that she too
can say "NO"
and that she has
the power to disagree
and to assert her personality.

This chapter shows
how dads are affected
by this dramatic transition
where his little princess
has become
a little
more
complicated.

Inside this Chapter

Observations from 101 Dads of Daughters

- The Terrible Two's—Ah Yes!

Terrible Twos—Ah Yes!

She Had This Huge Spirit In This Little Body—Of Course She's Going To Scream

"People say there's the terrible twos. Well, I thought they were the wonderful ones, the terrific twos, the thrilling threes, the fantastic fours. She was creative. She had a light in her eyes. She was courageous. She would walk on walls, you know, four feet up when she was two or three years old.

And yeah, she was bossy. She knew her mind and she wanted her stuff. But she was also very respectful and she had lots of friends.

I thought everything was easy. Even when she was throwing temper tantrums, I didn't get all hyped on it. I was like, 'Oh, here's this huge spirit coming into this little body. Of course, she's going to yell and scream.'

My experience of her is that she was absolutely perfect. I absolutely loved everything about her."

Lucas, fifty year old kindergarten teacher, father of a twenty-five year old daughter (divorced when his daughter was four but stayed one-hundred percent involved throughout her entire life)

Strong Willed At Two Years Old—Yikes! I Thought Only Teens Are Like That

"Okay there's a good story. Two years old, she's leaving a room that I'm in with her. She throws something down on the ground [because] she's upset with me or something like that. I don't know what. [So] she's walking out of the room and I tell her, 'Get back in here and pick that up.'

She turns around to look at me and goes, 'No', and turns around to walk away. I say, 'Hey, get back here and pick that up.' She turns around and goes, 'No'. She turns a little and then walks away again.

So I use an even stronger voice, 'Stop right where you are. Now you get back in here [and] pick that up right now.' She takes a step back and looks me straight in the eye and goes, 'No,' and walks away.

Then I pick it up myself.

That's not fair! She's two years old. She can't be a teenager already {he laughs}."

Ron, forty-seven year old school counselor and father of an eleven-year-old daughter and a twin eight-year-old daughter and son

If We Could Channel That Strong Personality—It Would Serve Her As An Adult

"Up until about eighteen months my daughter was a quiet little girl—beautiful, perfectly well developed and doing all those normal things.

Then, between eighteen and twenty months she started developing this hellacious terrible-two's temper. She was gonna take over the world.

> How different dads dealt with the terrible twos was fascinating.
>
> Some saw it negatively, as a reflection on their inability to control their child, a sign of impotence in a way.
>
> But others saw it positively, as their daughter's momentary exhibit of her strong will, a period that soon passes.

She would have pretty strong bouts of temper and anger, and would have to spend a lot of time in her room—because rather than sit there and have an argument with her, that was our choice of discipline.

[We basically said], 'Okay, if you can't be decent in the presence of people, you're going to just spend time in your room.' We would [give] her the old 'time-out.'

That was probably for a good year-and-a-half to two years.

We refer to [her] as a strong willed child. She wanted to have her way and she would express herself very strongly.

But as we were raising her, my wife and I both knew that this was going to serve her well if we could sort her through this. Because that's indicative of a very strong personality, that was going to be great when she's grown up.

But right now it has to be channeled.

So that was a conscious decision on our part, to discipline her— not harshly, but to not allow her to [get taken over by it].

You know, that's what kids are like sometimes. I mean, I don't recall feeling angry with her or whatnot. There was some frustration, 'Oh here she goes again.' But, I don't recall just being frustrated beyond belief. It was kind of like, 'Wow, I hope this doesn't last too long,' [he laughs].

But we discussed it as parents. We were aware that this was something that we needed to parent her through rather than just give up and throw up our hands.

The thing that worked for her was just isolation. She's very social so that was a very good punishment.

I don't think spanking would have been an appropriate one for her. I mean, it happened on occasions where she [got] the quick, 'You've got to stay out of the street,' and that kind of thing. But it wasn't by any means a very common way of discipline for her.

[It really helped that my wife and I] were on the same page in regards to how to deal with her. Most of the time it was, going to her room or restricting her from environments where she was expressing herself inappropriately.

Eventually, she got [that behavior] out of her system and so, she was a delight as a teenager."

Richard, fifty year old male nurse anesthesiologist, father of a twenty-five year old daughter and two sons

Some Surprises from this Chapter

Dads with a Two-Year-Old Daughter

- **Terrible-Twos:** No surprise that many dads were frazzled by their daughter's outbursts and tantrums during this terrible-twos period.

  Although most dads survived virtually unscathed, dads with control issues seemed to have the greatest difficulty interacting with a daughter through this assertive phase.

  For these dads, responses generally ranged from their imposing a regimen of strict rules and guidelines on their daughter *("...nipping it in the bud")*, to their checking out emotionally *("I can't handle this!!!")* – a state that would last a lifetime for an unfortunate few.

- **This Great Energy:** The real surprise came from the many dads who saw their daughter's assertiveness as a positive – a demonstration that this was a child with a huge spirit in a tiny body, *("...so of course she is going to scream at times")*.

  The explanation that, *"helping her harness this energy would help my daughter become a great force as she became an adult,"* was a positive that many dads expressed.

Stage Four: Age 3-5 – Socialization

– Big Things Come In Small Packages –

Defining Factor: She learns to socialize (how to act in public), gains friends, learns how she fits into her family (is she loved and important) and how she fits into the world (her self esteem).

In this chapter
dads tell how this little person
who has come into his life
is leaving an unexpected
emotional imprint.

Inside This Chapter

Observations from 101 Dads of Daughters

- This Is Such A Fun Age—We'd Have Real Conversations
- Daughters Say The Most Amazing Things
- My Daughter Loved Being Dramatic
- The Divorce Was Rough On My Daughter

- Young Kids Are Like Sponges
- Every Child Is Different When It Comes To Potty Training
- My Daughter Was In A Hurry To Grow Up
- Little Kids Sometimes Go Exploring And Get Lost
- As A Dad I Really Had To Make Time For My Daughter
- As A Dad You've Got To Be Patient—But Sometimes It's Tough
- And Then—There Are Those Fun Moments With Your Daughter

This Is Such A Fun Age—We'd Have Real Conversations

My First Encounter With This Two-Year-Old Girl Was Very Interesting

"At two [my stepdaughter] was pretty precocious, pretty friendly. She had a bounce in her step, a ready smile.

[One time when I was picking her mom up for a date] we had a conversation about what she was interested in and what she did in school—I think it was kindergarten.

It was a very interesting conversation. Here I am, a twenty-five-year-old man having an interesting conversation with a two-year-old while I'm waiting for her mother to get ready. It was kind of fun.

She was well adjusted and happy, with her aunts [living with her] in the apartment. They all had a really close knit relationship. So [my stepdaughter] Kiana was pretty well adjusted."

Bill, forty-six year old human resources manager of a Fortune 500 company, father of a twenty-six year old stepdaughter and a twenty-one year old son (he came into his daughter's life when she was two)

We'd Have Fun Conversations—Like Best Friends

"She's always been so much fun to be around.

And it's funny because no matter how old she is, I always end up saying the same thing to her, 'Kaylin, I've been waiting your whole life [for you] to be this age.' {laughing}

Yeah, so she's always been fun to be with.

You could hold a conversation with her when she was so little. She just wanted to have conversations with you. As soon as she was able to, you could sit and talk and talk and talk. It's just like best friends.

So yeah, as a young child she was easy to get along with and to be around. Always happy in her playing."

Ken, 9/11 New York City fireman and father of a six year old daughter and two sons

When I'm In The Mountains My Phone Rings—'Daddy I Miss You'

"Yeah, when I've gone up to the mountain to staff [men's work] trainings, my wife will call me and she'll say, 'Your daughter wants to talk to you for a second.'

[When my daughter gets on the phone] she'll say, 'Hey daddy, I'm really sad for you.' She'll be crying. That's her way of saying, 'I miss you a lot.'

It's so moving. Oh God, it's such a moving experience."

Ray, forty-eight year old computer executive, father of a five year old daughter

Daughters Say The Most Amazing Things

Sometimes My Daughter Would Say The Most Beautiful Things

"{He laughs} With Liz, she was a very expressive child. [I remember] she was looking out the back window in the kitchen. Happy to see a rainbow out over the hills, she said, "Thank you God, that's a pretty rainbow."

[That] just blew us away, you know, out of the mouth of babes."

Many dads described this as the greatest period.

Experiencing a child as she evolved into a real person was magical.

There was a joy in having conversations with this young child who was fascinated by her new world.

Carl, sixty-five year old ex-music teacher, with forty, thirty-eight and thirty-six year old daughters (divorced twenty years ago but stayed involved as their dad)

My Daughter Tried To Comfort Me In My Moment Of Sadness

"[When my mom died] it was very sad. [My daughter] Iman was probably four years old, so she knew something had happened.

I explained to her what had happened to her grandmother, my mom. I remember when we were coming back from the grave site, we were in the limo. She was sitting on the other side, and she said, 'Dad, I know you're sad because your mom died, but I'm still here.'

And I tell you, up until that point I was holding it together really well. But when she said that, I just... I just kind of broke down. Yeah."

Darryl, forty-seven year old business executive, father of a seventeen year old son and a fourteen year old daughter

My Daughter Loved Being Dramatic

She's Such A Drama Queen

"My daughter is a drama queen. Absolute drama queen, always has been."

Ron, forty-seven year old school counselor and father of an eleven-year-old daughter and a twin eight-year-old daughter and son

I Was So Proud—Watching Her On Stage When She Was In Daycare

"There was one event where [my daughter's daycare was] putting on a show.

The lights get dark, the big curtains open up, and there is Jacqueline, just [four] years old. She's dressed up like Cher, with a microphone in her hand.

She's singing, lip syncing literally. She knows the words to the song. I forget {which song}, one of the Cher songs that was popular at the time. And she's walking back and forth.

I was in tears, I was so proud of her. I mean she was the only one up there. Her daycare teacher was below the stage walking back and forth with her just in case she would fall.

I just remember everybody going nuts, just clapping and going crazy for this {four}-year-old lip syncing Cher. That's how I knew I was in trouble.

{He laughs} So all the acting and now she's in voice lessons and acting classes. Yeah, that's one of my first just truly proud memories of her as a kid."

Craig, thirty-nine year old father of a ten year old son, eight year old daughter and fifteen month old son

She Came In Screaming When She Saw Blood

"She was always a little hysterical.

She was riding her bike, fell off her bike, comes in screaming because she saw blood on her knee. Eventually we were able to wipe the blood off. {It turns out} it wasn't her blood, it was somebody else's blood.

So she was always a little hysterical about stuff."

Len, sixty-eight year old attorney, father of a thirty-five year old son, a thirty-four year old daughter and a twenty-eight year old stepdaughter

The Divorce Was Rough On My Daughter

I Wasn't There For My Daughter The Way I Would Be Today

> "It was rough. I moved out and {my daughter} wasn't happy about it. She was really angry and really scared.
>
> {Unfortunately} I think I wasn't the father that I wish I had been. What I mean is, I was there for her, but I wasn't there for her the way I would be and have been these days."
>
> *Carl, fifty-nine year old M.D. and director of an international non-profit organization, father of a twenty-one year old daughter (divorced when his daughter was four but stayed involved as a dad)*

Young Kids Are Like Sponges

My Daughter Was Really Into Music—The Instruments… The Singing

> "{He laughs} My daughter loves musical instruments.
>
> I remember one time after I was out of the military I took her to a concert. She was about three-and-a-half-years-old and she was telling her daddy about the different instruments that she saw on stage. For a three-year-old that was remarkable.
>
> {So I} brought all these instruments home, and she knew what each one was.
>
> She was very, very interested in the musical part of it. She started on flute and then also played oboe. She also was a very fine singer and still is.
>
> See, I'm in music. I'm a music teacher so that was a very unique {opportunity} {he laughs}."
>
> *Carl, sixty-five year old ex-music teacher, with forty, thirty-eight and thirty-six year old daughters (divorced twenty years ago but stayed involved as their dad)*

Every Child Is Different When It Comes To Potty Training

My Three Kids Were So Different

"[My three kids] are very different {he laughs} My oldest daughter was forcibly potty trained at five. My son was potty trained around three or three-and-a-half. My youngest daughter potty trained herself at two-and-a-half."

Ron, forty-seven year old school counselor and father of an eleven-year-old daughter and a twin eight-year-old daughter and son

My Daughter Was In A Hurry To Grow Up

My Daughter Always Wanted To Keep Up With Her Older Sister

"[As a young child my daughter Jennifer] worked very hard to keep up with her two older sisters. There was no back seat. She was right there with them all the way. We lived on a small school campus, and every once in a while we'd have a hard time finding Jennifer. So finally—it was usually my ex who would call the elementary school and find out that Jennifer was in class with her sister. The teacher didn't mind that much at all, 'Oh, that's not a big problem.'

> The experience is different when she has an older sister or brother who is close in age.
>
> The younger daughter seems to develop social skills faster and is often in a greater hurry to grow up.

{He laughs} We did send Jennifer to a pre-school which helped her get ready for school—because she wanted to go so much. She was anxious to grow up quickly."

Carl, sixty-five year old ex-music teacher, with forty, thirty-eight and thirty-six year old daughters (divorced twenty years ago but stayed involved as dad)

Little Kids Sometimes Go Exploring And Get Lost

We Searched For Hours—We Almost Called The Police

"I remember the time when {one of my daughters} got lost. We {searched} for a couple of hours and were about ready to call the police {when} we found her asleep in a closet. They were playing hide and seek and she fell asleep in a closet. {We were} very happy that we found her fine."

Carl, sixty-five year old ex-music teacher, with forty, thirty-eight and thirty-six year old daughters (divorced twenty years ago but stayed involved as their dad)

As A Dad I Really Had To Make Time For My Daughter

She Didn't Have A Sister To Play With, So I Spent Lots Of Time With Her

"I think because she didn't have a sister, {when her older brothers} were off doing boy things, she was content playing {by herself} with the dolls.

Which probably drew me even closer to her. I couldn't just tell her, 'Go play with your sister,' like I could tell the boys. So she's just sitting there alone.

Now if you're sitting there alone, I was going to make sure that you're not lonely.

{A parent} can't be that busy. What could be that important that, while {she} sits there and feels lonely, {you're not going to spend time with her}?

I was fortunate enough to have spent a lot of time with her. Her toddler years I was her main care giver. My wife was at work and I was at home with her {because of my shift work}.

I layed on the floor and played with her and read with her and bathed her and fed her and changed the diapers."

Ken, 9/11 New York City fireman and father of a six year old daughter and two sons

Even When I Spent Time With My Daughter, My Mind Was Somewhere Else

"I was focused on work, focused on stuff.

Even in the times she was with me—[after the divorce] we were doing every other weekend and then I had her for a night or two during the week—but even on the weekends when I had her, I fault myself for not devoting as much time as I wish I had to just hanging with her."

Carl, fifty-nine year old M.D. and director of an international non-profit organization, father of a twenty-one year old daughter (divorced when his daughter was four but stayed involved as a dad)

As A Dad You've Got To Be Patient—But Sometimes It's Tough

How Could I Be So Impatient With My Little Girl—I Started Hating Myself

"[Most difficult about my relationship with my daughter] is my patience.

Sometimes I'll have explained about six times how to draw the letter 'a' or I'll explain this technique on how to do her homework and she won't do it. She just struggles with it and struggles with it and struggles with it.

[But] I don't know how to say this any differently so I feel myself getting impatient. Then I start piling on myself, like, 'What kind of father gets impatient with his five-year-old daughter?'

Then I start hating myself. It just adds on to the frustration. Then I don't feel like I'm loving her, I feel like a jerk. I don't want to feel like that. It's tough."

Ray, forty-eight year old computer executive, father of a five year old daughter

And Then—There Are Those Really Fun Moments With Your Daughter

It Was So Much Fun Going Camping With My Daughter

"One of the things that stands out for me is that my daughter enjoyed being outdoors in the wilderness, and {so did I}.

When she was very young, just starting to walk, her mom and I did a backpacking trip in the Gila wilderness in New Mexico. We put a child carrier pack on top of my backpack and I carried her.

> This is the age where a dad can be involved in memorable activities with his daughter.
>
> Even dads with few memories of their daughter growing up can generally recall some fun outing, camping trip or road trip with their daughter.

I remember how much fun she had, walking around and around the tent, just holding onto the side. If she fell, she could fall into the tent.

On later trips, one of the fun things was—we had this huge sack that we put the sleeping bags in. I don't quite know how we put the game together, but at some point she crawled into this big bag and I would spin her. I mean I'd put her in the bag, close the bag and then spin her {he laughs}. Sort of like a merry-go-round with me as the merry go round.

She couldn't stop laughing. She just loved doing that."

Carl, fifty-nine year old M.D. and director of an international non-profit organization, father of a twenty-one year old daughter (divorced when his daughter was four but stayed involved as a dad)

I Do Really Fun Stuff With My Daughter

"For my daughter's fourth birthday party, we had a big treasure hunt through the woods with her friends. I ran out early and set out these various clues at the walk-through. They would find the clues and the clues would lead to a piece of treasure, yeah!

Just two weekends ago we did a sunrise dash to the sea. We'd get up at two in the morning, take some friends of hers and blow down to the beach. We'd watch the sunrise, hang out for a few hours and then come back.

That's just apparently a rage among her friends, the sunrise rampage."

Andrew, forty-six year old schoolteacher, father of two daughters age nine and ten

Drawing What We Talked About—A Great Way To Connect With My Daughter

"[What does my daughter remember most about growing up?]

Hmmmm. Probably I would say, learning to draw with daddy because we'd spend a lot of time drawing whatever we'd talk about. Whatever we're talking about, we'd grab a piece of paper and start drawing. She's in the middle of making two books now.

I think it's a great way [to connect with your daughter]. Whatever you're talking about, you can stay focused on it for a lot longer if you're drawing a picture about it. Then you can evolve a whole conversation about it, and make lessons that are going to stick a lot longer because [otherwise your child] has a short attention span.

If you do something like that, they can focus a lot longer because they're working on it.

Last night we were just sitting in the living room. She came over with a few pages stapled together and she says, 'I'm making a little book.'

So I says, 'What is this book going to be about?'

So she says, 'What do you think it should be about?'

So I says, 'Why don't you make it about the things you like to do?'

So we made a list of things she likes to do. Then she counted the pages and she said, 'Okay, I have seven pages, I need seven things to do.' So we wrote seven things that she likes to do. Then she drew a picture for each thing on her scrap paper and now she's putting them into the book.

Tonight she was just sitting in her bed and she drew probably another four or five pages. She drew a castle, she drew the four seasons, she drew a picture of me and her inside a heart!

So if you asked her what she remembers about growing up, [it's] probably drawing pictures with daddy, because that's what she'd do a lot."

Ken, 9/11 New York City fireman and father of a six year old daughter and two sons

Some Surprises from this Chapter

Dads with a Daughter Age Three to Five

- **At Last, Full Conversations:** One surprise was how important this period was for so many dads in cementing a lifelong relationship with a daughter.

  This was the first time a dad and his daughter would engage in full conversations. He got to play teacher and mentor to a daughter who was receptive and appreciative (sometimes for the last time in her life), and that was deeply meaningful to many of these dads.

- **The Importance of Interactive Activities:** During this period even dads with difficulty communicating seemed to connect with their daughter through sports, camping, car trips, school projects and other activities. Shared experiences during this period would be fondly remembered even by dads in their seventies and eighties.

- **Patience:** No surprise here. Finding enough time and patience for a daughter was still an issue for many dads, as it remained for some throughout much of their life.

  Dads who were finally ready to spend time with their daughters later in life, often found a relationship that was difficult and awkward because the groundwork had not been laid during these earlier years.

Stage Five: Age 5-12 – School

– Teachers, Books and Dirty Looks –

Defining Factor: She learns how she fits into school, sports, band and organized activities (social status).

She also learns discipline and institutional rules (sitting quietly in school and not speaking until allowed).

Between school
and after-school activities
the connection to dad is changing.

During this period some dads
feel a sense of helplessness
as friends and foes
emerge for his daughter
and there's little
daddy can do about it.

In this chapter
the connection to his daughter
is strengthened for some dads
through meaningful conversations,
homework and sports,
while for others,
there is a profound sadness
as the emotional gap
with his daughter widens.

Inside this Chapter

Observations from 101 Dads of Daughters

- Now That My Kids Are Older I Interact More With Them
- I Love My Daughter's Ability To Express Her Feelings
- Girls Just Wanna Have Fun!
- We Made Sure Our House Was Fun And Safe For Kids
- Without A TV My Kids Got More Creative

- My Job Allowed Me More Time To Spend With My Daughter
- My Experience With Her Kindergarten Class Was Great Fun
- As She Was Growing It Became Harder To Do Things Together
- Once We Found Things To Do Together—It Was So Much Fun!

- My Daughter's Mood Swings Could Sometimes Be Hard On Me
- There Are Moments When I Wish I Had More Patience
- As A Guy There Are Some Things I Will Never Understand

- My Daughter's First Ride On A School Bus Was A Big Deal
- Her First Day At School Was Traumatic For Me—Alone In Our House

Continued...

- I Have Fun Memories Of My Daughter's School Projects
- My Daughter Had Lots Of Friends At School
- Her Dealing With Mean Kids At School—That Was Tough
- At School My Daughter Got Used To Families Getting Divorced

- My Daughter Is Coming Into Her Sexuality—That's Terrifying
- As She Goes Through Physical Changes—Our Interaction Is Changing
- Now There Are Times My Daughter Doesn't Want Dad Around
- To Raise A Powerful Woman—I Needed To Set Boundaries

- A Girl Doesn't Follow The Same Rules As Everyone Else
- Her Mom And I Sometimes Disagree Over Rules For My Daughter
- Moms And Dads Play Different Roles In Raising A Daughter

- I Bury Myself In My Work—It's Hard To Talk About My Feelings
- As A Guy I Need To Listen Better

Now That My Kids Are Older I Interact More With Them

I Really Didn't Start Appreciating My Kids Until They Were Five Or Six

"For both of my children, I think I really appreciated them more when they got older. Not as little babies. I would say five, six. That's when I started really appreciating them."

Leonard, seventy-three year old ex- school music teacher, father of a forty-six year old son and a thirty-three year old daughter (divorced later in life but has stayed close to his daughter)

I Love My Daughter's Ability To Express Her Feelings

My Stepdaughter Connected More With Me As She Got A Little Older

"[As my stepdaughter approached her teen years], oh yeah, I noticed—well I mean, she was opening up and becoming more confident.

She was fairly shy when I first met her."

Terry, sixty-two year old engineer and father of two sons age thirty-eight and thirty-four, a stepson age twenty-four and a twenty-one year old stepdaughter

My Daughter Lets Me Know If I Hurt Her Feelings—That Really Helps

"I love her empathy. I love her ability to express her feelings.

I love when she tells me that I hurt her feelings. Even if I don't like it, I love [that] she's willing and able to let me know. I mean it's great."

Ron, forty-seven year old school counselor and father of an eleven-year-old daughter and a twin eight-year-old daughter and son

Girls Just Wanna Have Fun!

Let Your Toenails Get Painted—You'll Get Voted 'Best Dad Ever'

"I got voted 'best dad ever' when [my daughter's friends] saw that I allowed her to let my toenails get painted. That was the deciding factor of 'best dad ever.' So a great dad is somebody that lets his toenails get painted."

Lucas, fifty year old kindergarten teacher, father of a twenty-five year old daughter (divorced when his daughter was four but stayed one-hundred percent involved throughout her entire life)

> For many dads this was a highly interactive period with their daughters.
>
> She is just beginning school, making new friends, and stepping out into the world.

My Daughter's Greatest Memories Are When We Went Fishing, Camping, Biking

"On Memorial Day we used to go to a camp-out with the group that I had been associated with. Every year they'd get together and go camping up in Sinking Springs, doing the fishing and the running around in the woods, and just the overall camping experience.

I [used to] ride motorcycles, but since I've been in school and since [my daughter's birth] I really haven't had the chance to get a bike up and running.

[But] I got a bike up and running one day. I was just seeing how roadworthy it was, and she asked, 'Can I have a ride?' Much to her mother's chagrin I put her on the back with the helmet on, and just ran up and down the street about twenty-five miles an hour.

She talks about that, 'When will we go riding again?' She's constantly asking, 'When are we going camping? When are we going fishing?' So she's got a good memory of that."

Rob, forty-eight year old truck driver going to night school for massage therapy, father of
a ten year old daughter and a twenty-three year old son (from a previous marriage who he
also remains involved with)

I Love That She's So Ticklish

"I don't think my daughter has a non-ticklish bone in her body
{he laughs} and that brings a great joy. All my kids have their
spots, but this child—everything is ticklish for her still, and I
love that about her."

Ron, forty-seven year old school counselor and father of an eleven-year-old daughter and a
twin eight-year-old daughter and son

My Daughters Were So Much Fun To Be Around

"I remember one day when our youngest was in eighth grade, the
three girls and I went to a fashion store in the mall in Albuquerque.

All three of them needed to have full length gowns for a banquet
that was coming up. [Of course] none of them had [anything] in
their closets, so they wanted something new.

So the girls tried on dresses for me. That was just absolutely
incredible, to sit there and watch the girls. They were listening to
me as far as style and everything else. We just had a blast.

I had fun with those kids. They were just absolutely delightful.
They would sing together and… {he laughs}

…Sometimes when they were fighting over dishes and that kind
of stuff, I would just walk into the kitchen, take the silverware
drawer and drop it in the dirty water. Which meant they'd have
to wash all the silverware, put it in the drawers and all that. So
after a while if they heard my footsteps, they would automatically
start singing {he laughs}. That was cool, you know."

Carl, sixty-five year old ex-music teacher, with forty, thirty-eight and thirty-six year old
daughters (divorced twenty years ago but stayed involved as their dad)

We Made Sure Our House Was Fun And Safe For Kids

Kids In The Neighborhood Felt Comfortable Playing In Our House

"We had a room in the basement that we'd clean like once a month. It was the play room where the kids played. Just about everybody in the neighborhood played down there. And you know, they were safe, they were behaved, and they felt comfortable. That's the way I wanted my home to feel.

The kids could have played at other homes, but those other homes didn't allow kids to build the huts out of blankets and all that kind of stuff. I think that's an important thing for kids to be able to do."

Carl, sixty-five year old ex-music teacher, with forty, thirty-eight and thirty-six year old daughters (divorced twenty years ago but stayed involved as their dad)

Without A TV My Kids Got More Creative

Our TV Broke So The Kids Were Forced To Find Other Activities

"We spent about three-and-a-half to four years with no television in the house. It broke and we decided not to get it fixed. So [instead] we played games, we read stories and sang songs together. That was really wonderful.

As a result, my kids love to read. [My daughter] Heather studied piano. My youngest is a fine guitarist.

And that all began then. I believe that for sure."

George, seventy-five year old father of fifty-two year old daughter and two sons; also later became stepfather of another daughter (when she was a teenager) and a stepson

My Job Allowed Me More Time To Spend With My Daughter

Shift Work Allows Me To Spend A Lot Of Time With My Daughter

"[As a fireman] we work twenty-four hours at a time—two twenty-four-hour [shifts] a week. So you have a lot of time to be dad.

It's great. Because of the shift work you get to spend a lot of time at home. You're a chaperone on every field trip. All the kids in their class know you. You're the cool dad because you're always around and part of everything. You're there to take them to school and you're there to pick them up from school and you're part of everything they do.

[My daughter] knows that she's lucky and that I'm lucky, [the fact that] we've gotten to spend so much time together. The girls in her class don't get to spend the kind of time she gets to spend with her daddy. So she feels as lucky as I feel—that she has a daddy that gets to spend as much time with her as I do."

Ken, 9/11 New York City fireman and father of a six year old daughter and two sons

I Suddenly Had More Time For My Kids—When I Stopped Being An Airline Pilot

"The first couple of years pre-divorce, when I was doing the business stuff, I was there all the time. I was [no longer a pilot] on a crazy airline schedule, so I coached my daughter for soccer the first three years.

> Some dads actually changed jobs so they could spend more time with their daughter during these early formative years.

I had a neighbor who said, 'Hey, is Savannah going to play soccer?' I'm like, 'Sure, what do we do?' She goes, 'Well, your daughter signed up and I signed *you* up for coaching.' So I coached Savannah when she was like four, five, and six-years-old. I probably coached for five years of soccer.

I do a lot of stuff like that. I do Boy Scouts for my son. That's a different story, but I've done that for four years. So yeah, I coached her quite a lot. I love coaching her and she likes it. She looks up to me and loves having me coach. It's quite a gift [that I am able to spend that time with my kids]."

Mark, forty-four year old Navy pilot, father of a fifteen year old daughter and an eleven year old son (divorced when his daughter was seven but stayed involved as a dad)

My Experience With Her Kindergarten Class Was Great Fun

When I Was Reading To Her Class—I Got This Funny Nickname

"[When my daughter was in] kindergarten, parents were invited to come read a story to the class. So I left work to read a story to her class. I was all exited. I love reading stories to my kids and other kids.

I get in front of the class and the teacher says, 'Will you introduce our speaker to the class.' [My daughter] says, 'This is daddy,' and [everyone] starts laughing.

[So] the teacher says, 'No, no, no, no. Mister…' And [my daughter] goes, 'This is Mr. Daddy' {he laughs}.

Now I'm Mr. Daddy. You can call me MD—a medical doctor? No. Not in this house. In this house, [MD stands for] Mr. Daddy {he laughs}. I love being a daddy. I love even more being Mr. Daddy."

Ron, forty-seven year old father of an eleven-year-old daughter and a twin eight-year-old daughter and son

Being Around Kindergarten Kids Brings Out The Seven-Year-Old In Me

"When we go to the classroom to help the kindergarten teacher, we don't just work with our kid, we work with all the kids. It's really beautiful because I hear [my daughter] say, 'That's my daddy,' to the other kids. She has such pride and joy, you know what I mean.

I don't see [other] parents doing the stuff that I do when I go there. The kids were all chasing me around the playground. I had like, twenty-five kids chasing me around the playground.

The other day the kindergarten teacher said, 'Wow, I've never seen that.' She brought out her camera and got pictures of twenty-five kids chasing this dad around the playground.

I play basketball and surf, so I'm pretty athletic. I can toy with five-year-olds in terms of running around with them. I'm not saying I'm ready for the Olympics, but I'm saying that I really enjoy being active with kids. I get down to a kid level.

I may be forty-eight or forty-nine or whatever the hell [age] I am, but I think somewhere down there I'm still about seven."

Ray, forty-eight year old computer executive, father of a five year old daughter

As My Daughter Was Growing It Became Harder To Do Things Together

Her Middle Years Were More Of A Challenge To Find Things To Do Together

"The biggest challenge I think [was] particularly during those the middle years, when [my daughter] got to be about eleven or twelve up until she got into college. I think that's a more challenging time to find activities that you can do together."

David, sixty-three year old real estate appraiser and Vietnam vet, father of a thirty-seven year old son and a twenty-nine year old daughter (divorced when his daughter was eight but stayed very engaged with his children growing up)

But Once We Found Things To Do Together—It Was So Much Fun!

I Remember One Summer Just The Two Of Us Going On This Fantastic Car Trip

"One summer I drove out with Nadja. She was five or six or something like that. We had the greatest time. She just enjoyed that so much.

We sang songs. I worked at a blues song about, 'There's a crow sitting by the side of the road,' and we would just add lyrics to it. I would add a lyric and she would add a lyric and we'd sing the chorus and we'd keep going. Both of us just loved that trip.

There was one point, I guess it was Nevada, and there was a huge storm we could see brewing maybe fifty miles off. We just watched that storm come towards us, and the sky get darker, and lightening. It was a fantastic experience just driving into that storm. That was a delightful trip that we took together."

Charlie, fifty-ish father of a twenty-seven year old son and twenty-five year old daughter (his wife died in a car accident when the kids were young. He has always been close to his kids)

Doing the Father-Daughter Weekends With My Daughter Really Connected Us Together

"I think if you were to talk to [my daughter] about 'daddy' moments, it would absolutely be going to Wisconsin for the father/daughter weekend and the first time we ran it in New York. She's already talking about next August and what's going to happen next year.

For dads who tried them, organized father-daughter weekends and events were great fun.

Dads who participated often commented that the memories from this shared experience would easily last a lifetime.

I remember it was a chance for her to spend real quality time with dad. We took a flight to Chicago, rented a car and then drove out to Wisconsin.

I give her a ton of credit at six years old. You know, these are strangers in a strange place. I remember the first couple of hours, her just clinging to my thigh. I was surrounded by [some familiar faces] so I felt very much at home. But she was six and scared, so I was very [available] to her in those moments.

After a couple of hours, the actress started coming out in her. She created friends very quickly with all the girls that were on the [camp] site.

I remember sitting back with some of the men and just watching the daughters play. I remember her running up and asking for permission, 'Can I go here with so and so.'

I just remember how safe she felt after all that initial fear in this place. The hayrides with her, the horse rides with her, making masks with her. We made masks of each other's face as one of the events.

She almost grew up in the three days—from the fear that she had to, 'Wow, I'm embracing this freedom.' It was a great, great event.

I remember coming home on the plane and—the girls made twizzles [which was] jewelry they made out of string that the fathers attach to their ankle or whatever. I remember I had one on my ankle.

Well she took some of the extra yarn from the site and was making another one on the plane. She was so into it, and she goes, 'This one is a special one.' So when she fell asleep on the plane I took it and put it on my ankle.

I remember how angry she was when she woke up. I heard 'special one' thinking, oh great, it's for her dad. Well, silly me. It was for herself. But now it was on my ankle and it still is there to this day. Every time she sees it, it's part smile, part anger, you know, 'That was meant for me, dad!' But it was a great event.

Then watching her the next year, helping teach the other girls how to make the jewelry. She felt like she was a little bit of a leader. It was great. It was amazing.

I recommend [the father/daughter weekend] to every father and his daughter no matter what age, if you can get your daughter there.

– Spending That Kind of Time With Her Really Opened Our Communication –

[I've] seen over the last couple of years how—for lack of a better word—how stubborn [my daughter] can be. She's really strong-headed at such a young age, and sometimes communication becomes very difficult. So for me, [because of] these specific events with her, it's so much easier to communicate with her.

I've got to try to figure out how I take [more of that magic] back to the real world. But I'll look at her sometimes and I'll call her 'Time-Like-Bunny,' because everybody comes away with an animal name after the weekend. And I'll say, 'Time-Like-Bunny, you're not living up to your animal name here.' And she'll give a chuckle, 'Come on, Charging-Rhino.' She calls me by my animal name.

It's created a connection and a bond that, when we talk about it, it's almost like this sacred place. So it's a very special place that we have. She teases her brother about it, of course. [So now] he gets upset we're not going to any father/son weekends."

Craig, thirty-nine year old father of a ten year old son, eight year old daughter and fifteen month old son

The Summer Trips With My Daughter Were Happy Times

"[I remember the] trips, yeah. At the time I was teaching on the East Coast [so] every summer we would drive back to New Mexico to visit my family.

I remember camping along the way. Those were happy times. I had more time to be with them, you know. Also they had cousins to play with."

Leonard, seventy-three year old ex- school music teacher, father of a forty-six year old son and a thirty-three year old daughter (divorced later in life but has stayed close to his daughter)

My Daughter's Mood Swings Can Sometimes Be Hard On Me

She's Like Hot And Cold Running Water At Times—It's Rough

"There are times that [my daughter] doesn't want to be hugged, and that's fine. Then there's times like the other night, where I was already in bed and she came in and snuggled up against me. I asked her, 'What's up?' She said, 'We don't get to snuggle a whole lot.'

I was almost asleep when she came in and did that, and [then] I was wide awake just enjoying the snuggling. Little things like that.

She's at that age where sometimes it's like, 'I don't want to be touched by my parents or whatever.' [Then] we hold hands, we cuddle, we just kind of sit on a couch and watch a movie together.

It's almost like hot and cold running water at times. I try to allow for things like that and not take it too personally, but that's sometimes very rough. I mean, it's like, I'm on my way up to bed and I want to give her a hug and a kiss goodnight and she walks away from me. That's gut wrenching at times.

I'm trying to give her a little bit of security even though I might need it myself too. Hug the wife goodnight, [then] try to hug the daughter and she's walking away, and it's like, 'Damn, wonder what's eating her or what's wrong. Is it something I did? Is there something going on at school'—the what-ifs or what's-going-on type questions that make you feel insecure. That's the roughest part."

Rob, forty-eight year old truck driver going to night school for massage therapy, father of a ten year old daughter and a twenty-three year old son (from a previous marriage who he also remains involved with)

There Are Moments When I Wish I Had More Patience

If I Had More Patience For Her Whining, I Could Resolve Conflicts Easier

"My youngest is the drama queen. She cries probably at least once a day [from] something that's upsetting her, particularly if she's having some big fight with her mom. Then I can be the one that goes in there and tries to calm her down and comfort her, and give her the hug she needs and help her get through it all.

This was a common theme…

Many dads voiced tremendous guilt because they were not always patient enough with their daughters.

[What I find] most difficult is staying empathetic to her drama—figuring out when it's really real and when it's just over dramatized.

It's not just the drama. It's the whining that often accompanies it. So being able to tell when the tears are just her [being dramatic] and when they're sincere real tears, [that's a challenge].

I mean, they're all real for her. But if I take every one of those tears as, 'Oh no,' I'm gonna be going, 'Oh no,' everyday, and I just I don't think that serves anyone well in this family including her. So that's a big challenge.

When she's not in that whiny mode, I think she's such an easy kid. I do. It doesn't mean she doesn't have the challenges, but her being a sweet empathetic loving kid, it's really easy to love on her.

She's my most physically affectionate kid, and most receptive to [that affection] too. Plus I have a connection though sports with her, which I don't necessarily have with my other kids. That's fun too.

[But it's] the whining that gets me. Sometimes it's no big deal, but other times I lose patience with her. My wife's definitely got more patience with her.

[If I had more patience] I think, rather than get angry and raising my voice at times to her, I would probably just set limits on it, and isolate her until she stops the whining. We could end it quicker. [That would be] one way to try to break her of this habit—because it wears on everyone in the house."

Ron, forty-seven year old school counselor and father of an eleven-year-old daughter and a twin eight-year-old daughter and son

As A Guy There Are Some Things I'll Never Understand

Sometimes You Just Accept That You Will Not Understand Why She's Mad

"Like any relationship, you have to read [the situation] and react and adjust accordingly.

[For example] there were times where my daughter was mad at me for reasons I couldn't even figure out. So you have to make a choice.

Sometimes I remember trying to confront her [with], 'What is wrong with you? Why are you acting this way?' And other times you learn that—you know what? It is what it is. It's something I will not really understand nor should I press her for an answer to it. You just leave it alone."

Bill, forty-six year old human resources manager of a Fortune 500 company, father of a twenty-six year old stepdaughter and a twenty-one year old son (he came into his daughter's life when she was two)

My Daughter's First Ride On A School Bus Was A Big Deal

She Was So Excited About Her First School Bus Ride

"[My daughter's first day of school] was exciting for her. She had watched her brothers go on the big bus for a couple of years now, and [finally she's thinking], 'Am I going to get to go on the big bus?' So it was very exciting for her."

Ken, 9/11 New York City fireman and father of a six year old daughter and two sons

Her First Day At School Was Traumatic For Me—Being Alone In Our House

Coming Home To An Empty House—That Was Tough

"[My daughter's first day at school] was traumatic for me. I felt a great loss, coming home after dropping her off at school.

Most of the time, I'd drop her off at school just to have the extra time with her in the mornings. [That way] things could be calm and easy and she could get to school in a good frame of mind—as opposed to putting her on that frantic bus where everybody's screaming. [Instead of] getting to school all frantic, she's getting to school in a good frame of mind.

Anyway, dropping her off and then coming home to the empty house, you [say to yourself], {he whispers} 'Where's my little girl? My little girl's not a baby any more. She's not a baby.' {almost crying} That was a tough day. Those were tough days. But you get used to everything I guess, after a while."

Ken, 9/11 New York City fireman and father of a six year old daughter and two sons

I Have Fun Memories Of My Daughter's School Projects

What Kind Of Music Do Hamsters Like—Ask The Cat

"[I remember] the time she did a science experiment trying to determine what kind of music affected hamsters. She had one hamster cage that was tuned in to hard rock, rock, and all that kind of stuff, and another cage in a different room that was listening to classical music all the time. What was funny was that we kept losing the hamsters because we also had a cat {he laughs}. Whenever we needed to find the hamster, we'd follow the cat and usually find the hamster."

Carl, sixty-five year old father with forty, thirty-eight and thirty-six year old daughters

My Daughter Had Lots Of Friends At School

My Daughter Has A Very Good Mothering Sense

"As she was growing up, she was very well loved by everybody at school—good kid, very bright, very willing to help people out. She has a good mothering sense."

Carl, sixty-five year old ex-music teacher, with forty, thirty-eight and thirty-six year old
daughters (divorced twenty years ago but stayed involved as their dad)

Her Dealing With Mean Kids At School—That Was Tough

I Learned That Sometimes I Need To Listen Without Trying To Fix Anything

"Mean Girls—I think probably one of the toughest periods that my daughter Iman and I have gone through. I personally had to do some research and read some books on this myself to try to understand what I call the 'mean girl syndrome.'

> One of the most painful and complicated issues for many dads was dealing with mean kids at school.
>
> The dilemma came from a dad's wanting to protect his daughter without damaging her socially.

She has a group of friends that— and it's been better in the last year—but we went through about six or seven months where every day it was an emotional crisis because one of the girls in the group didn't like her, or said something about her, or texted someone about her.

The world was pretty much coming to end. She wanted to drop out of school, go to another school, et cetera. My daughter was emotionally upset to the point where she literally made herself ill and had to miss school for several days around the stress level.

I didn't go through anything like this with [my son], so I just couldn't wrap my [mind around it]. My first reaction was for her to just ignore these girls. Get a new set of friends. But that was the wrong answer. I found out I needed to listen [rather than trying to fix it]. I wanted to fix it, but my daughter really just wanted me to listen. She didn't really want me to fix it.

I have the same problem with my wife too. I've learned that sometimes she just wants to tell me [something]. She doesn't want me to fix it."

Darryl, forty-seven year old father of seventeen year old son and fourteen year old daughter

This Girl At School Had Targeted My Daughter As Her Arch Enemy

"She has talked to me a couple times because one of the girls at school is, in my daughter Joanna's terms, her 'arch-enemy.' It's very emotional because the girl has chosen Joanna as her arch nemesis, arch enemy for a number of years over absolutely nothing.

Joanna at times has needed some support and some encouraging words that I've been able to give to her at that point [whenever she was affected by this]."

Rob, forty-eight year old truck driver going to night school for massage therapy, father of a ten year old daughter and a twenty-three year old son (from a previous marriage who he also remains involved with)

I Think My Daughter Was Secretly Happy That We Stood Up For Her

"I'm [pretty sure my daughter Kiana] would remember the times where both her mother and I stood up for her. This might have been in junior high school [when] other kids would pick on her. Kids sometimes would be mean, as kids sometimes are.

There was a time where she was interested in comic book cards. They're like baseball cards but of comic book heroes.

Well she had her whole binder full of comic book cards that she was really proud of.

One day she had taken it to school and some of the boys in her class took them from her and hid them, and told her they weren't giving them back.

She came home upset and crying. She told us that she talked to the teacher and the teacher did nothing. So the next day my wife and I showed up at the school and walked into the classroom. The teacher, you know, looked frightened for a minute. We kind of took over the class.

Again, I'm not sure I'm too proud of this to be honest, but it is a memory.

We said to the class, 'We're Kiana's parents. Some of you have taken her cards. We want to know who it is.'

Three of them meekly raised their hands. We asked them to step outside into the hallway so we could ask them where the stuff was.

It was a bit more drama than was necessary, but at the time we felt that she was being taken advantage of and the teacher didn't do anything about it.

I'm sure she was a bit embarrassed. But to be honest, I also got the sense that she was happy that her parents would go to those lengths to protect her."

Bill, forty-six year old human resources manager of a Fortune 500 company, father of a twenty-six year old stepdaughter and a twenty-one year old son (he came into his daughter's life when she was two)

At School My Daughter Got Used To Families Getting Divorced

So Many Kids In Her Class Had Gone Through Divorce—She Almost Expected It

"My daughter went to a small Catholic school in La Jolla from kindergarten through eighth grade, so she was there for nine years.

One of her good friends had already gone through a divorce. And of course, the statistics [for divorce are] fifty percent—probably in the Catholic school maybe only thirty percent of the parents are divorced, but that's enough.

She's with the same kids every year. Out of a class of thirty-five, maybe ten of the kids are from divorced families. In fact, one of her friends was one of the earlier ones to go through it and more followed.

It was tough on her at first [but eventually she got used to it]. It's hard."

Mark, forty-four year old Navy pilot, father of a fifteen year old daughter and an eleven year old son (divorced when his daughter was seven but stayed involved as a dad)

My Daughter Is Coming Into Her Sexuality—That's Terrifying

My Daughter Is Not Quite Interested In Sex Yet—That's A Relief

"[Has the issue of sex come up?] Yes. When my wife was pregnant with my son, questions started coming up from my older son, 'How did mom get a baby inside of her?'

So I actually purchased 'The Miracle of Life', one of these books that are geared towards children. [Then I] sat [my son and my daughter] down on the couch and proceeded to go chapter-by-chapter as the pregnancy went month-by-month.

My daughter lost interest around chapter three. She could basically care less. The conversations were a little, I guess, over her head.

But having the older brother who is now eleven going on twelve talking about—you know, girls, and reading about things in books—the conversations are there.

So I'm not, uh... I went into scientific detail around the pregnancy, and I didn't, uh, uh...

I still tell her to this day that whatever you hear from your friends or from school, if you have questions, don't get the answers from them. Know that you can come to me or come to your mom and talk to us about anything. That's been the focus more than [anything else].

She did ask about 'what's a period' because she heard about a period at school. But not really boy-girl kind of stuff yet.

She says she has boyfriends. 'I have Nick, my new boyfriend in school,' that kind of stuff.

To me it's a question of teaching her to come and talk to me if she has questions, as well as just [to show her] a respect, like the respect her mom [was shown when she was a child]."

Craig, thirty-nine year old father of a ten year old son, eight year old daughter and fifteen month old son

How Is My Daughter Learning About Sex—That's What Scares Me

"She's nine years old. I think in this day and age, at nine years old, kids are coming into their sexuality earlier. She'll be watching a TV show and she gets embarrassed if I'm around because there are boys kissing girls. It's embarrassing for her when I'm there.

The issue of talking to your daughter about sex was terrifying for many dads.

It seemed to represent the end of innocence.

Suddenly she was no longer his *little* girl.

She doesn't watch a lot of TV. What TV she does watch, it's episodes on Netflix [on a computer]. We don't even have a TV in the house.

[So] yes, I have absolute apprehensions about it. I'm terrified.

It goes back to that whole idea of—[because I have a daughter] I've got to worry about every single penis on the planet.

I mean, I'm a boy. I know how often I think about sex.

So yeah, I have apprehensions about it. I have apprehensions about how she's going to learn about it. I have apprehensions about what boys she's going to like, and if I'm going to like the boys that she likes.

I'm very concerned about how she's going to learn about sex, and who she's going to be having that first kiss with, and what that's going to be like. I mean, the stories I hear [are disturbing, of what goes on, even] at their birthday parties. That's not something that I really want my daughter participating in.

[Of course] when I say she's coming into her sexuality, I mean it's so minor compared to other children that have been exposed to a heck of a lot more media than she has been exposed to.

Still, last year—it was third grade—she came home [and] we found a little notebook of her drawings. The drawings were of people having sex. The drawings were of kids around the computer watching people having sex on the computer.

Now these were very concerning images for us. We have never been able to find out where those images came from. In our home we have severely limited her access to computers and we have no pornography in our house.

I can't say that I've ever been to a web porn site, but [even] her access to my computer is extremely limited.

So the only thing we can think of is that she was at a friend's house, and the friend had a computer or the friend has an older brother who has a computer, and somehow she saw these images.

It was very upsetting. That was one of those times when she would not tell us where those images came from. She didn't feel like she could be open with us. She said they just came in from her imagination.

I'm hoping she's going to be able to say no to [those types of influences] or realize [if something's] not a good choice to make.

So yeah, [I'm very concerned as she's getting older]."

Andy, forty-six year old TV reporter, father of a nine year old daughter (recently divorced but remains close to his daughter)

I Explained That Boys Are Stupid—They Can't Handle That Bikini Stuff

"You know, we talk a lot about boys. Many times I'm the one who initiates the boy conversation. I explain to her, 'I see some of the swimsuits that you wear in our backyard. You will never, EVER wear those any place else but in our backyard. Do we understand each other?'

[I explain to her], 'It's because boys are stupid. I am a boy so I understand that. As we get older, we become more mature. But when we're fourteen, fifteen, we're really stupid. We can't handle all that bikini stuff. We just can't handle it, okay, because we are stupid. So those swimsuits will never leave our backyard. They just will never leave it.'

We also talk about the fact that [my daughter] Iman and I go out on father-daughter dates, for lack of a better word. [I do it to show her that], 'When a boy wants to interact with you, this is how you should be treated. They should open the door for you, they should do these other things. That's what a *real* young man does.'

We also talk about examples of young men that she should *never* think about bringing to my house because it's just not going to fly with me. Pants sagging down, you know, all this stuff. No, we're just not going to tolerate that, so don't even bring him into my house. Just not going to happen."

Darryl, forty-seven year old business executive, father of seventeen year old son and fourteen year old daughter

As A Divorced Dad—I'm Not There When Boys Show Up To Date My Daughter

"Once my daughter got into high school and dating, I was not [interacting as much with her]. It felt like I was sort of pushed away in a sense.

Of course, as a divorced father, I'm not there at the house when the boy shows up to pick up my daughter. So that's probably the biggest hole, the biggest loss that I felt as a divorced father.

To some degree I was able to talk to her about [sex], and her mother was able to talk to her. We've even had subsequent conversations about it. [But] I'm still not fully comfortable.

[For example when] she and I go to a movie now, and let's say there's a very sensual, sexual scene. She seems to be very comfortable about it. It doesn't seem to bother her a bit, but I'm still uneasy about it. It's still a little bit difficult, particularly some of the sexual humor and, you know, naked bodies and all those kind of things.

I can tell the difference between me watching that with her versus watching that with my son or watching it with my wife."

David, sixty-three year old real estate appraiser and Vietnam vet, father of a thirty-seven year old son and a twenty-nine year old daughter (divorced when his daughter was eight but stayed very engaged with his children growing up)

I Have A Fear Around My Ability To Protect My Daughter If She Needs It

"She's a big flirt, a big-time flirt. So I've a lot of fear about how she will be and what situation she might get herself into, and my ability to protect her. That's a fear."

Ron, forty-seven year old school counselor and father of an eleven-year-old daughter and a twin eight-year-old daughter and son

As She Goes Through Physical Changes—Our Interaction Is Changing

Our Relationship Is Changing As My Daughter Grows Into Her Womanhood

"Now that she's growing into her womanhood, the relationship does change. She's got issues that dad only knows about peripherally, that mom is better to talk to about.

Obviously she's not coming to you saying, 'Oh look dad, I got my first period.' At least that didn't happen with me.

> For some dads this was a somewhat sad time.
>
> It marked the end of physical playing.
>
> He could no longer physically horse around with his little girl.

I mean, to a certain extent it has to change, right? She isn't sitting on my lap as often. So yeah, I think things certainly change from that regard, both physically and also emotionally."

Bill, forty-six year old human resources manager of a Fortune 500 company, father of a twenty-six year old stepdaughter and a twenty-one year old son (he came into his daughter's life when she was two)

My Daughter Was Less Comfortable Hugging Me After She Started Developing

"Um, uh… [my daughter's] development of breasts was not a subtle deal. I mean, she developed fairly large breasts at a fairly young age. It did have an effect and uh… my sense was that she, well…

When she was little, we used to be really physical. We'd do a lot of roughhousing and wrestling.

One of her favorite games was, I'd put a big bedspread over me and play monster. I'd rummage around the room and, you know, just sort of envelop her in the bedspread like a big amoeba or something.

That stuff changed when she started to develop breasts. My sense is that she was less [comfortable with the physicality]. She didn't give me the same kind of full body hugs that she used to. I would say that's still true even now.

I mean, every once in a while if there's something emotionally dramatic that happens, I'll get one of those hugs. But [generally] it's more of, you know, the A-frame hug?"

Carl, fifty-nine year old M.D. and director of an international non-profit organization, father of a twenty-one year old daughter (divorced when his daughter was four but stayed involved as a dad)

I Realized My Daughter Was Growing Up—That Made Me A Little Sad

"You know, we basically didn't have any locks on any rooms in the house. So we'd be in and out of the bathroom with each other, and changed in front of each other.

Then, about eleven or twelve, all of a sudden she needed to set a boundary and she wanted to be modest around dad. All of a sudden, I couldn't watch her change from clothes to PJ's, and I couldn't' be in the bathroom when she went to pee.

It was a non issue, it was no big deal. Then all of a sudden at eleven, twelve she needed her privacy and she needed to express her modesty.

It made me feel a little sad, but I [also realized], that's good. It's time for her to grow up. She's growing up."

John, fifty-six year old schoolteacher, divorced father of eighteen year old daughter (divorced when his daughter was seven but remained close to her)

There Are Times My Daughter Doesn't Want Dad Around

Even Though She Needs Her Privacy—I Want Her To Know I'm Still There For Her

"I feel like my daughter can talk to me. She asks {all kinds of} questions.

But I think there are times now when she does feel embarrassed and doesn't want dad around, that she needs privacy.

So I try to give her that. But I'm also trying to let her know that I'm still there for her."

Andy, forty-six year old TV reporter, father of a nine year old daughter (recently divorced but remains close to his daughter)

To Raise A Powerful Woman—I Needed To Set Boundaries

I Encouraged My Daughter To Follow Her Dreams

"I wanted to raise a really powerful, independent woman. So I was always thinking—in kindergarten, what did she need here in order to be a really powerful woman—and when she was in fifth grade what did she need here. So I was always holding that vision in my mind.

> This issue of setting boundaries was interesting.
>
> Some dads seemed powerless to control their daughter.
>
> Others were quite comfortable setting a few rules and sticking to them.

I also encouraged her to be great, to be 'in her greatness.' I encouraged her to follow her dreams, whatever they are.

I used to tell her, 'You're going to be a really powerful woman. I don't know what you're going to be as far as, you know, president or homemaker or nurse or artist or whatever. I just know you are going to be a powerful woman.'

When she was little, I gave her a lot of boundaries {but} in a loving way. Then as she got older I just released her into who she is.

I think that's what makes a great dad. That's what made me a great dad."

Lucas, fifty year old kindergarten teacher, father of a twenty-five year old daughter (divorced when his daughter was four but stayed one-hundred percent involved throughout her entire life)

A Girl Doesn't Follow The Same Rules As Everyone Else

I Try To Get My Daughter To Clean Her Room—She's Too Busy Drawing Butterflies

"{Big sigh} The hardest thing is trying to get my daughter to keep her room cleaned.

{He laughs} You know, I could do her laundry, wash it, dry it, fold it, put it in the basket. {Then I tell her}, 'You know where all your drawers are? I've been through this with you a hundred times. Can you put all this away?'

'Okay daddy.'

Then you go back in there — it just happened tonight. She was laying on the floor. She has a little step-stool to get up into her closet {so she can} reach the hangers. But on that step-stool is butterflies and dragonflies and lady bugs. She's got her book open and she's drawing all those bugs in her book.

I said, 'I need this wash basket in order to do the next load of laundry. You have to put this stuff away.'

{He starts laughing} So she dumped the clothes out on the floor, left the wash basket by the front door {and she tells me}, 'Okay, there you go. There's your wash basket.'

So the clothes I had just washed are on the floor and she's happily back to drawing in her book—a very beautiful butterfly and a beetle and a lady bug and a dragonfly. They're all drawn in there, and the clothes are on the floor."

Ken, 9/11 New York City fireman and father of a six year old daughter and two sons

It Gets Really Frustrating When My Daughter Doesn't Listen To Me

"There's frustration in the moments when I'll ask her to do something like seven times and it doesn't happen. It's just like she doesn't care that I'm talking to her.

The whole homework analogy—I start getting impatient and I start getting this tone and I'm feeling sarcastic.

Then I get sad, about what kind of dad treats his daughter like this. It's a father whose patience is pretty much gone at this point and needs to take a moment to regroup. That's the kind of man this happens to.

It's tough. I think women can relate to that as well."

Ray, forty-eight year old computer executive, father of a five year old daughter

Her Mom And I Sometimes Disagree Over Rules For My Daughter

My Ex-Wife And I Had Different Ideas Of What Was Acceptable For Our Daughter

"As my daughter got older, dealing with issues of curfew, what kind of clothes she could wear, what she couldn't wear, how much uh, how much

It drove some dads crazy that mom sometimes had different parenting rules than they did.

Daughters who recognized these differences could periodically play one parent against the other.

Many dads admitted they were susceptible in trying to buy their daughter's affection.

cleavage she could show—that's one of the things I remember coming up as a conflict point between her mom and me. Would I enforce the same rules {when she visited me} in Oregon that she had {at home} in Tucson?

{He laughs} There were times when {my daughter} Lea told me that her mom wouldn't allow her to wear something like that {when my daughter knew it was no big deal for me}".

Carl, fifty-nine year old M.D. and director of an international non-profit organization, father of a twenty-one year old daughter (divorced when his daughter was four but stayed involved as a dad)

Moms And Dads Play Different Roles In Raising A Daughter

She Gets Emotional Support From Her Mom—But I'm Also There For Her

"At this stage, most of the support my daughter's getting is from her mother. She does a lot more of the emotional communication with her mother right now.

But I try to be there if she needs me or if her mom is not around. {For example} there are times when she's not feeling well, and where I'm the only one there. {During those moments she} is very receptive to my support and caring.

She also loves it when I cook. I'm a good chef."

Rob, forty-eight year old truck driver going to night school for massage therapy, father of a ten year old daughter and a twenty-three year old son (from a previous marriage who he also remains involved with)

I Bury Myself In My Work—It's Hard To Talk About My Feelings

The Father-Daughter Training Is Helping Me Escape From My Isolation

"I have a tendency to crawl into the isolation of a laptop computer when work is getting too unbearable.

When my daughter is vying for my attention and I really can't give it, I will [at least] try to stop what I'm doing and explain what's going on, 'You know why daddy can't do this right now...' or 'This is what's happening.'

I don't [spend enough time with her] probably as often as I should, let's put it that way.

['Father-daughter' training weekends helped]. The conversations like, 'I love you most when...' and, 'I get very angry when you...' conversations like that, and then explaining the 'why' behind it.

So we have had talks and conversations like that, more-so when I'm either on the weekends [with her] or just come back from a training."

Craig, thirty-nine year old father of a ten year old son, eight year old daughter and fifteen month old son

As A Guy I Need To Listen Better

I Try To Fix My Daughter's Problems—And That's Not What She Needs

"Sometimes I just need to listen and not try to fix the problem. I have become much better at that I think.

[For example] the 'mean girls' experience. [It caused my daughter Iman to have] an emotional breakdown kind of thing. That was tough, I've got to say.

[Unfortunately, because I wasn't so great at just listening] I tried to enlighten Iman.

[But] Iman is more of a leader than a follower. [On her own she told the mean girls], 'You don't like me? Tough! I'm on to my next thing.'

I think that was a valuable lesson [watching her take care of that for herself]. That's the part that really surprised me."

Darryl, forty-seven year old business executive, father of seventeen year old son and fourteen year old daughter

Some Surprises from this Chapter

Dads with a Daughter Age Five to Twelve

- **The Beginnings of Rejection:** It was surprising how quietly painful this period was for so many dads. After finally learning to connect emotionally with his daughter, she was now beginning to step out on her own, to have her own friends, to be taught by teachers and coaches other than dad.

  Even horsing around, physical play and hugs were suddenly different. No more goodbye kisses in front of her friends. No more having dad around when she was with her friends.

  And those mood swings... They just made it more complicated for some dads *("One minute she loves me, the next she hates me. I cannot even begin to try and understand it...").*

- **A Loss of Influence:** The issue of school bullies and mean kids was complicated. A few dads came to a daughter's rescue. But for the rest, the inability to protect a daughter at school was unnerving.

- **Beginnings of Sexuality:** The landscape became complicated for many dads as their daughters entered puberty. A few dads were comfortable discussing sex, but for most, this was yet another not-so-subtle barrier to openly communicating with their daughter.

- **Listening Skills:** The best observation from this section was dads learning to listen rather than trying to jump in and fix everything. Simple advice, but difficult for many dads to practice without plenty of help and reminders.

Stage Six: Age 13-16 – Peers

– No Longer Daddy's Little Girl –

Defining Factors: She distances herself somewhat from her parents as she learns to define herself as a unique person not defined by her parents. She may not want her parents to be with her when she is with her friends.

For many dads this is
the age of
pubescent self-consciousness
where his daughter
no longer wants a kiss goodbye
especially in front of her friends.

In this chapter
some dads struggle
with rules and boundaries for his
ever-more-independent daughter.

Many of these dads also face
uncomfortable first discussions
about sex and boys.

Inside this Chapter

Observations from 101 Dads of Daughters

- My Daughter Was Entering Puberty—I Noticed Subtle Changes
- My Daughter Suddenly Wanted More Freedom
- I Feel A Little More Isolated From My Daughter These Days
- She's Not Moody Every Day—But She Can Get Pretty Emotional

- And Then—She Started Getting Interested In Boys
- Did I Talk To My Daughter About Sex...
- It's Scary How Some Kids Are Sexually Active So Young
- My Daughter Has Had Some Very Positive Influences
- Friends And Peer Pressure Were A Strong Influence
- I Have A Pretty Good Relationship With My Daughter
- We'll Even Talk About Her Menstrual Cycle If She Wants

- I Work Hard To Be A Good Dad—But It's Not Always Easy
- It's Been Difficult For Me To Connect Emotionally With My Daughter
- My Daughter Is Noticing That I'm Much Easier To Be With Now
- I Love Being A Dad To My Daughter

My Daughter Was Entering Puberty—I Noticed Subtle Changes

Once Her Older Sister Was Gone, She Suddenly Had A Bigger Responsibility

"Because our oldest had left and was off to college, [now] Liz was the oldest daughter in the role of responsibility, taking care of the house [while also taking care of] *her* life and boyfriends and all that stuff."

> *Carl, sixty-five year old ex-music teacher, with forty, thirty-eight and thirty-six year old daughters (divorced twenty years ago but stayed involved as their dad)*

> The realization that she was no longer daddy's little girl was unnerving for many dads.
>
> For the first time, the influence of friends was conflicting with the influence of dad.

My Daughter Wouldn't Kiss Me Anymore When I dropped Her Off At School

"She was always my little girl. She used to always give me a kiss before she got out of the car when I dropped her off at school. [Then] I think seventh grade, she wouldn't do that anymore.

But she promised me she would always be my 'little' girl. We had that conversation, I remember that."

> *Mark, forty-four year old Navy pilot, father of a fifteen year old daughter and an eleven year old son (divorced when his daughter was seven but stayed involved as a dad)*

My Daughter Developed Early—She Was Often Mistaken For An Older Girl

"You know, thirteen, fourteen. She developed early physically and so she frequently was mistaken for a much older girl. And she carried herself that way."

> *Richard, fifty year old male nurse anesthesiologist, father of a twenty-five year old daughter and two sons*

Her Friends Are Growing Up Quicker—She's Still More Of A Little Kid

"My daughter is starting to be more interested in older girl stuff. Yet she's still very much a little kid. She has friends that are moving there quicker but she's not. She's more of a little kid. That's just her."

Ron, forty-seven year old school counselor and father of an eleven-year-old daughter and a twin eight-year-old daughter and son

Puberty And High School—Yes My Daughter Is Going Through Changes

"{He laughs} My daughter Savannah really didn't change until about a month or two ago. She's probably a year and a half into puberty. I mean, you know, she first got boobs maybe a year-and-a-half ago, and she just started high school {so a lot of things are changing}.

She really wanted to go to this private Catholic high school. Her mom was totally against it—{well maybe} not totally against. Her mom said, 'You can go but I'm *not* going to pay for anything.'

My financial situation is very tenuous and it was very difficult, but I got her into the school through financial aid and through, you know, getting my parents to help out.

She was so excited, and very joyful and very positive. Then she was in the school for like two weeks and decided she didn't like it. It's been interesting."

Mark, forty-four year old Navy pilot, father of a fifteen year old daughter and an eleven year old son (divorced when his daughter was seven but stayed involved as a dad)

Once She Became A Teenager My Daughter Put On A Lot Of Weight

"My daughter put on a lot of weight {when she became a teenager}. She's suffering with obesity and stuff like that. She's working very hard on it, but it's been difficult for her. She's like me in that, because both of us are heavy."

Carl, sixty-five year old father, with forty, thirty-eight and thirty-six year old daughters

She's Not My Little Girl Anymore—It's Tough… When She Puts On Those High Heels

"The hardest thing for me with Iman is that my little girl is growing up. She's earned more privileges and more freedom but I tell you, it's hard for me to let go. It's hard for me when she wants to go out at night.

She's not dating, to my knowledge anyway. She goes out like—it would be four girls go out with four boys. And she dresses fairly conservative because she knows there's certain clothes that there is no way she is leaving my house with. But she may go someplace and change clothes [even though] she comes back in with the same clothes on.

So she's growing up, I mean, and she has those long legs! And when she puts on these heels and stuff, I'm just like… she's like a young woman, not like my little girl. {He laughs} So I'm struggling with that. I must admit I'm struggling with that."

Darryl, forty-seven year old father of seventeen year old son and fourteen year old daughter

My Daughter Suddenly Wanted More Freedom

She Wanted Her Own Room In The Basement

"She wanted a room very much to her own. The only one that we could figure would be to fix up a room in the basement where we were living.

{He laughs} She did a very good job with it, in spite of the black little spi-

As they entered puberty, many daughters wanted more freedom.

Some dads felt a sense of abandonment during this period.

ders and other things down there. She tended to live down there and all that."

Carl, sixty-five year old ex-music teacher, with forty, thirty-eight and thirty-six year old daughters (divorced twenty years ago but stayed involved as their dad)

It Didn't Really Bother Me When My Daughter Started Dating

"I had no problem with {my daughter's dating}. Not at all.

I just had the thing y'know, with her being home by a certain hour, initially anyway.

I didn't like them going places where they were going to stay overnight or anything like that. I was a little bit strict in that manner. I never let her do that until she was in college.

But it didn't bother me at all really. I had no problems with it."

Denis, fifty-six year old accountant, father is a twenty-four year old daughter and a twenty-eight year old son

My Daughter Likes To Stay Up Late And Sleep In Late

"[My daughter] is here right now in her room, still sleeping as teenagers so often do, hours at a time. She likes to stay up late and sleep all day."

Ed, fifty-one year old realtor, father of a fifteen year old daughter and two sons (divorced when his daughter was older to reduce the trauma he and his wife experienced, both being children of divorce)

I Feel A Little More Isolated From My Daughter These Days

Sports—I Wish I'd Had That Kind Of Time With My Daughter

"I wished my daughter was more into sports. I wished I had that game-playing thing with her. And it saddens me to see how hooked into electronics she is."

Ron, forty-seven year old school counselor and father of an eleven-year-old daughter and a twin eight-year-old daughter and son

Now That My Daughter's In High School I Don't Get To Coach Her Anymore

"I coached my daughter last fall, but she's in high school now so there's not much {coaching anymore}.

These days I'm often away {because of my returning to be an airline pilot}. If I'm home, I talk to her. She calls and I'll talk to her every day.

When I'm home, if I want to get together with her, there's no problem. My ex-wife is pretty cool about that. Yeah, so if I'm home now—let's say I have a vacation week or something, if I'm not working but it's {my ex-wife's} week {to have my daughter} and Savannah has got a volleyball game or something, I go to the game. I get to see her."

Mark, forty-four year old Navy pilot, father of a fifteen year old daughter and an eleven year old son (divorced when his daughter was seven but stayed involved as a dad)

She's Not Moody Every Day—But She Can Get Pretty Emotional

My Daughter Would Go In-And-Out Of Moods—For No Apparent Reason

"Oh, boy! I think we hear kind of in caricature, about the teens, the twelve-year-old, the thirteen, the angry phase where nothing is right and you're not smart anymore as a parent and she's not happy and blah, blah, blah.

Well yeah, {for my daughter} that started around eleven and I think that she—my daughter

> A daughter's mood swings were brutal on some dads.
>
> Those who didn't try to figure it out seemed to fare best.

is twenty-six now—so I think it ended probably on Wednesday {he laughs}.

I'm sorry, I'm sorry {laughing harder}. Not quite Wednesday but it lasted for a long time, to be honest. I mean, not every day is moody. But just the going in and out of moods for not a whole lot of good reason. One hour you're happy and we're having jokes and everything is good. Then I see you in the hallway an hour later and you've got the puss face on and nothing's right and everything's wrong with the world, kind of thing.

That probably set in [when she was] about eleven, twelve, until I would say about nineteen, twenty. And even then we have flash-backs {laughing}."

Bill, forty-six year old human resources manager of a Fortune 500 company, father of a twenty-six year old stepdaughter and a twenty-one year old son (he came into his daughter's life when she was two)

Despite My Daughter's Mood Swings, She Still Has That Great Free Spirit

"She goes through her 'mood swings' as I call it. [I mean] she can get into her diva mode. She is a ballerina and she gets into these modes about her artistry et cetera that, 'The world pretty much revolves around me.' It's a sense of entitlement.

But she's a teenager [and that's what teenagers do]. She still has that sweet spirit about her. She's still my conversationalist. No matter what day I come home, how long I've been gone, she wants to tell me everything that's going on with her and what's going on with some of her friends et cetera. I don't have to pull conversation out of my daughter Iman. Whenever we're in the car, we never have the radio on because my daughter is talking or asking me questions. We're having a conversation the entire time. So she still has a great spirit. She goes through her mood swings, but she's still that same free spirit she was as a little kid."

Darryl, forty-seven year old father of seventeen year old son and fourteen year old daughter

I Was Petrified—She Went Through A Total Meltdown Like In The Movie
The Exorcist

"This was the beginning of middle school, I think. [My daughter
Emily] really loved the [private school she had been going to]. She
loved her friends and loved being there. [But we didn't have the
money so we had to change her to the town school].

[Unfortunately] even though it was a small town [and she knew
many of the people], sending her to the town school did not sit
well with her. Then, totally out of character, one day she refused
to go to school. I'm talking about a full-blown meltdown—
screaming, yelling—I didn't recognize her. I was in shock.

I was at work [when] my daughter refused to go to school. My
wife didn't know what to do so she called the school to try to find
out if something had gone on there that would have traumatized
her. The principal of the school came over and my daughter just
went crazy, like full blown.

None of my other children have ever done anything like that, not
before and not since. I was petrified. I came home trying to talk
with her [but] it was almost like a demonic—do you remember
[the movie] The Exorcist. It was that intense. It was that intense.

Finally she stopped the screaming and carrying on and she said, 'I
don't want to go to that school. I want to go back to *my* school.'
[So] I just surrendered to her. I just stood there and I looked at
her and I said, 'Okay, I'll do whatever I have to so you can go back
there.'

I remember knowing in my heart it was not a logical thing [but]
it was the absolute right thing to do. It was not an issue of, 'Oh,
we can't afford it. You will go to the [town] school because I don't
have the [money].' I just [gave in and] said, 'No, you'll go there.
You'll go back there.'

The way I looked at it, somehow she figured out a way to get my attention about how important this was for her to be there, and I just said okay. And we did. We worked it out. I went and spoke to some friends and they sponsored her. They put up the money so that she could go to the school, and it all worked out.

And she absolutely loved the years that she went there, and did very well. She has always been a good student too, straight A student right through high school. Now with a couple of years of college under her belt she's [still] always straight A's."

Arthur, fifty-nine year old father of eight kids, including six daughters ranging from age fourteen to thirty-two

And Then... She Started Getting Interested In Boys

Guys Suddenly Became More Important To Her Than Dolls

"[When my daughter became a teenager] guys started becoming more important in her life than dolls. So she went through that phase of wanting to be pretty and impressive and attractive. She [also] tried to act tough because she thought, I guess, that's what gets the attention of the guys. [And] did it, yes. It got the attention of a [much older] twenty-year-old man [and that concerned me]."

Donnie, fifty-six year old father of a thirty-two year old daughter and thirty year old son (divorced when his daughter was eight but remained close to her)

She Started Wearing Makeup

"[My daughter also] started wearing make-up and all of that stuff, which was great. I loved it when she did that. But she still remained a tomboy. She's still a tomboy."

Denis, fifty-six year old father of a twenty-four year old daughter and a twenty-eight year old son

I Jokingly Play With The Idea Of Being The Kind Of Dad Boyfriends Are Scared Of

"[It's in] the TV shows my younger daughter is watching. Rather than Sponge Bob stuff, she'll now watch stuff like the shows where there's teenagers and they're dating and they're interacting and talking about cute boys and stuff like that.

My oldest [daughter] is a little delayed in that area socially. She looks older than her peers but she acts younger than some of her peers, so that hasn't really worried me yet. I've got a few more years before I have to start worrying about her really, in that regard. She'd much rather chase boys who want to run away from her, than do anything with the boy.

> For many dads, when their daughter started dating it felt like punishment in a way.
>
> They remembered how they had acted in their own youth so they knew what boys were after.

[Have I talked to her about sex?] No, it hasn't come up yet. I'm just trying to decide what type of dad I want to be around that. I jokingly play with the idea of being the dad that boys are scared of. I haven't taken the time yet to think about the effect that would have, those pros and cons.

I remember in my day the impact that had on some of the girls. But at the same time I think there is such a lack of respect these days—much more so than in my day—even for the repercussions from an adult that is feared. It may not be such a bad thing in this day and age, but that *was* a different time"

Ron, forty-seven year old father of an eleven-year-old daughter and twin eight-year-old daughter and son

Her First Love Lasted Years—After That It Was A Revolving Door

"[My daughter] Devan started dating when she was a junior in high school. She started going out with this guy for like, three years. He was a year older than she was. [After him], it was like, what letter of the alphabet are we up to now?' {he laughs} I can't keep track of how many [boys] she's gone out with."

Denis, fifty-six year old accountant, father is a twenty-four year old daughter and a twenty-eight year old son

My Daughter's First Relationship Ended Horribly—I Wanted to Hurt Him

"My daughter was sixteen when [her first serious relationship] started. [She met him when our family did volunteer work in Central America during the summers with our church. It was mostly a long-distance relationship] that lasted from sixteen to probably twenty.

Then, that one [relationship] fell out in a horrible way. He moved to the States and his values shifted. He changed and he broke her heart.

I wanted to hurt him—just the fact that he broke my daughter's heart, that he treated her poorly, that he didn't keep his word.

There was just something about him moving from Central America to the United States and being let loose in this culture. He didn't hold his values. He peeled off into the bar scene and the discos and...

So I was very disappointed and very defensive of my daughter. I was protective, defensive with a, 'Go ahead, make my day,' kind of attitude. I'd never do anything physically because he was in New York and I was here [in another city]. But I just remember being very disappointed and upset and thinking, 'How could he do this?'

And to hear her calling home and crying, that was really harsh too."

Richard, fifty year old male nurse anesthesiologist, father of a twenty-five year old daughter and two sons

My Daughter Made Bad Choices With Boyfriends—They Didn't Treat Her Right

"[My daughter's dating?] That was kind of hard sometimes, because she didn't always have the best judgment in some of the people she was dating. Some guys didn't treat her that nicely in my judgment.

She had one incident with a boyfriend she was dating for awhile, that she wanted to break up with. He got really angry with her and accosted her. We got a call that she was over at one of her friend's house. We called the police and had him arrested. He was put in jail. Actually, she was supportive [that we had been there for her]. I mean, she was, I think, grateful."

Terry, sixty-two year old engineer and father of two sons age thirty-eight and thirty-four, a stepson age twenty-four and a twenty-one year old stepdaughter

As A Divorced Dad—When She Told Me About Her First Kiss I Was In Shock

"[Because I was a divorced dad] I was not near my daughter during many of those phases in her life [when she was dating]. Basically my contact was by phone. I just used to see her during vacations.

I remember the first time she told me that a guy had kissed her. My approach to her has always been not to be judgmental, [but] I was in this kind of a shock that you know, that hit me in my gut. [Of course] I did not make any kind of remark. I just heard her and said, 'Okay that's good, okay. And how did you feel?'

So I tried to [make it seem like] I'm not judging, and open myself to what she wanted to tell me."

Jose, fifty-four year old therapist and television personality, father of a twenty-eight year old daughter

Pregnant At Sixteen Was Tough—Especially Realizing Her Life Was Up To Her

"[What was it like finding out my daughter was dating an older boy?] Well, I felt like it was her choice. [She was] sixteen to his twenty-one. That was five years difference, which really isn't that much difference of age, you know. I mean, she was definitely underage at sixteen when she got pregnant. But as you get older that five years difference isn't that much.

I don't know. I felt like her life was up to her to make the choices that she wanted to make, and have the consequences of her choices. If that's what she wanted then I was supportive of that."

Donnie, fifty-six year old father of a thirty-two year old daughter and thirty year old son

Did I Talk To My Daughter About Sex...

Luckily I Didn't Have To Talk To My Kids About Sex—Their School Did That

"Oh no no no. [I didn't talk to my kids about sex].

I don't know how old they were, probably around fourteen. My daughter Laurie went for her religious training, to get confirmed. They had a big conference or a big weekend where they talked about sex. That made it easy in a way, because somebody else had brought it up and dealt with it.

> It's funny how many dads used the word *trauma* when they described talking to their daughter about sex.
>
> If mom or school addressed the sex issue with her, that seemed to get many dads off the hook.

149

So I didn't [have to] deal with it. I mean, I never had any really great conversations other than in the context of, 'What was that weekend about?'

I'm sure my wife talked to her more about sex and stuff like that but I didn't have to deal with it. I mean, I wasn't afraid of to deal with it, but there was nothing, really, for me to be dealing with."

Len, sixty-eight year old attorney, father of a thirty-five year old son, a thirty-four year old daughter and a twenty-eight year old stepdaughter

It Was Traumatic For My Daughter—My Talking To Her About Sex

"In seventh or eighth grade, when my daughter was learning about sex, we would have time in the car and I would say, 'Okay, Kaja. I'm really uncomfortable with this [but] we're going to talk about sex.'

I knew she was growing away from me, you know, learning how to drive, her first date, staying out all night at theater parties and stuff.

I know she remembers the sex talks. They were really uncomfortable for her. She said that she started having trauma every time she knew I was going to talk about sex."

Lucas, fifty year old kindergarten teacher, father of a twenty-five year old daughter (divorced when his daughter was four but stayed one-hundred percent involved throughout her entire life)

I Have Not Had The Full-On Birds-And-Bees Sex Discussion—Definitely No

"Have I talked to my daughter about sex? I have not, no. I know her mother has. [But] not yet, I haven't talked to her about sex.

I have talked to her in some ways {he stammers uncomfortably}… I don't know what you mean about talking about…

I haven't talked to her the full-on version birds-and-bees sex discussion. But I have talked to her about being careful about putting herself in compromising positions. One, because it could be dangerous. It could lead to, you know, bad things happening, especially being around people that are drinking.

So I've talked to her about putting herself in compromised positions where it's *perceived* that she's doing something. I've talked to her about that a lot because people start rumors. She's very pretty, a great athlete, smart. She's got everything going for her {so} I have to talked to her about how people can be jealous and start rumors.

But I haven't really talked to her about sex, not sex acts. I just, no, I would have to say no on that. But her mom has talked to her about it."

Mark, forty-four year old Navy pilot, father of a fifteen year old daughter and an eleven year old son (divorced when his daughter was seven but stayed involved as a dad)

Maybe The Sex Discussions Have Started—My Wife Isn't Telling Me

"[When the sex discussions come up] what I hope is once that starts, that she'll be willing to listen when I engage her.

But my daughter's {definitely} gonna go to her mom, because my kids are much more connected to my wife than they are to me.

In fact, it may have already started and my wife just isn't telling me. It's possible."

Ron, forty-seven year old school counselor and father of an eleven-year-old daughter and a twin eight-year-old daughter and son

It's Scary How Some Kids Are Sexually Active So Young

I Need To Trust That My Ex-Wife Will Also Protect My Daughter

"I don't like my daughter going to movies without another parent being around. She thinks she's old enough to go to the movies with her girlfriends. But I just hear too many weird [things] going on these days, of what girls are doing in the movie theater with boys.

It's just scary, that kids are so sexually active at such a young age. I'd like to prevent her from that as much as possible but we all know that boys and girls are going to be boys and girls. I mean, I started pretty early when I was young.

A lot of it is supervision and knowing where your kids are. I try to make a point of it when I have her. I know where she is and I'm chaperoning. But as a divorced dad that's not always possible. It's part of my work, to release and let go and know that the ex-wife loves her and cares for her and is going to protect her as well."

Ed, fifty-one year old realtor, father of a fifteen year old daughter and two sons (divorced when his daughter was older to reduce the trauma he and his wife experienced, both being children of divorce)

When My Daughter Decided To Keep The Child—Her Own Childhood Was Cut Short

"My daughter ran through a rough period in her life. She was a little bit rebellious and became pregnant with my first grandchild when she was sixteen years old. She gave birth to a daughter, Tiffany.

She kept the baby and got married to a guy that was a little bit older than her. He was strong and opinionated, and I think that's what attracted her to him—except he's just confused about what it is to be a man, and to be the head of his household, and how you do that.

[Finding out my daughter was pregnant at sixteen] I can tell you that there was maybe five minutes of disappointment. But I asked her how she felt about that and they decided they would keep the child. She wasn't going to give it up for adoption or get it aborted.

[Of course] I felt that her childhood was going to change and that she was going to step into a different chapter in her life. But I felt in my spirit, confident for her that no matter what happened, she would be able to make it. I felt certain that God would take care of her."

Donnie, fifty-six year old father of a thirty-two year old daughter and thirty year old son

My Daughter Has Had Some Very Positive Influences

4-H Club Really Taught My Daughter Initiative

"We were living in a small rural town in Colorado at the time. We were very involved in 4-H (youth organization) and so my daughter was doing a lot. She did sewing [and all kinds of stuff].

The animal project was raising goats. She had the grand champion goat for the County Fair and things like that, so she was developing a lot of really responsible-type behavior.

> Introducing positive influences from a young age seemed to pay off big-time with many daughters.
>
> This seemed especially helpful when dad could participate in some of the activities.

Not that she liked doing it. But on her own initiative, she would get up and do animal care. She would do her sewing projects. She did very well at those and won a lot of awards."

Richard, fifty year old male nurse anesthesiologist, father of a twenty-five year old daughter and two sons

Sending My Daughter To Private School Really Helped Her—And Us

"My daughter's in a [Montessori-style] private school now. We've had a lot of issues with her from the moment she went to [public] school. She's always had trouble bonding with teachers [there]. When she was two-and-a-half, they were starting to wonder if she had selected autism.

[But getting her into] a nationally known, learning-difference educational school, that's been phenomenal for her. She's just really coming around there, whereas if she stayed in a public school she'd probably be failing and floundering and miserable, and we would be too.

For instance, most of the school's kids are dyslexic [which causes learning problems because they flip letters and words around when trying to read. However] dyslexic kids can learn to read and write if you start them on cursives rather than block letters. Block really messes them up. It's harder to flip things around in cursives, so they start with cursives.

They also have a lot of different ways of teaching kids to read, based on the specific needs of each kid. There are three different reading programs. You go in based on what your specific needs are.

[And there's] lots of passive reinforcement. I get emails all the time when my daughter does something really *good* that they want to highlight behavior-wise.

So I'm getting all these emails that she's very nice to someone, or that she's very active in the class, and that she engages in and participates in class, stuff like that.

I'm so used to [expecting] negative stuff [that] when I get something from school, I think she did something wrong, 'Oh my god, what did she do?' [But instead they tell me], 'Your daughter was commended for doing this and this,' stuff like that."

Ron, forty-seven year old school counselor and father of an eleven-year-old daughter and a twin eight-year-old daughter and son

Friends And Peer Pressure Were A Strong Influence

Junior High Was A Snake Pit Of Bad Influences—So We Home Schooled Our Kids

"[With] the schools in the area, we didn't like the way they managed their schooling and we felt we could do a better job at home. [So home schooling our daughter became] our preference.

> Those two words
> – peer pressure –
> sent chills to many dads.
>
> Some overcame the influence through home schooling.
>
> Others found that positive interaction with a daughter's friends was crucial to staying connected with her.

[For example, in the school] there were some social interaction that we could see developing. It was a small community so it's pretty hard to hide anything. We thought, you know, we don't want our kids to be stuck in that little cliquey stuff.

Especially Junior High was just a snake pit of [bad] behavior and it wasn't dealt with very well by the teachers. The way kids treated each other. They were just cruel as far as insults and comments and social ostracizing. So we thought, well, enough of that crap. We'll just bring our kids home.

[Also] our values were fairly conservative Christian and there were some things that we wanted to maintain at home that they weren't going to get at school."

Richard, fifty year old male nurse anesthesiologist, father of a twenty-five year old daughter and two sons

My Daughter's Friends Have Had The Greatest Influence On Her

"My daughter's really focused now on her friends. She's got great friends [so I think] she'd remember most hanging out with her friends at the beach and at school. She had a really great experience, from kindergarten through eighth grade. That's what she'd remember."

Mark, forty-four year old Navy pilot, father of a fifteen year old daughter and an eleven year old son (divorced when his daughter was seven but stayed involved as a dad)

With Peer Pressure She Suddenly Felt Like We Were No Longer Good Enough

"[In] junior high and high school My daughter got more sophisticated friends. [So suddenly she] decided we lived in the ghetto because all her friends lived in Huntington Harbor {nervous laugh}. Y'know she started being competitive that way."

Denis, fifty-six year old accountant, father is a twenty-four year old daughter and twenty-eight year old son

My Mom Found This Piece Of Paper With All These Cuss Words

"[Is my daughter getting involved with boys?] Yeah, oh yeah. She has a phone and so she's texting. She listens to songs that probably, uh, kids like to listen to that they shouldn't — they have cuss words in them. She's starting to feel her oats.

[In fact] she just actually got back from my mother's up in Oklahoma for summer vacation. She took one of her little girlfriends up there and my son also, twelve-years-old, went up there with them. The three of them stayed up there for a week or ten days with my mom.

My mom called me laughing the other day saying, 'I was cleaning up around the house and I found this piece of paper under the sofa. It was [loaded with] all these little dirty words.' Evidently they all had gotten together after my mom had gone to bed and they'd written down all the dirty cuss words they could think of {he laughs}.

That piece of paper—my mom had found it under the bed or under the sofa or something. She told me, 'I didn't want to say anything to them because I didn't want them to have that memory of me finding that piece of paper.' {That's why} I never brought it up to their attention."

Ed, fifty-one year old realtor, father of a fifteen year old daughter and two sons (divorced when his daughter was older to reduce the trauma he and his wife experienced, both being children of divorce)

As A Divorced Dad—She Wanted To Hang Out With Her Friends And Not With Me

"When I got a divorce from her mother, I would have my daughter every weekend. {That was} until she got to the age to where she wanted to stay in town and hang out with her girlfriends instead of going with me into the farm on the weekends."

Donnie, fifty-six year old father of a thirty-two year old daughter and thirty year old son (divorced when his daughter was eight but remained close to her)

I Have A Pretty Good Relationship With My Daughter

It's Okay To Talk About Feelings Even If Uncomfortable—But I Don't Overdo It

"My daughter calls me every day and we talk a lot. {I think} we have a great relationship, more than {just} a father-daughter relationship, I like to model for her what it's like to be an authentic compassionate person—{that} it's okay to talk about feelings and share parts of yourself.

> Not every dad was comfortable talking to his daughter about relationships and feelings.
>
> Those who pushed past the discomfort seemed to be more approachable as a father.

When stuff is brewing {with her}, I step into my sovereign {dad role} and we sit down and we have a talk. We have good conversations, {sometimes} talking about things that are uncomfortable.

She may not like it and she may be uncomfortable {so} I don't push it. But I do let her know it's okay to talk about feelings and talk about things that are uncomfortable. {Generally} she'll talk about it to a point, then she'll say she's had enough and we let it go.

It's interesting. I was talking to her mom the other day and we were having a deep talk, which is kind of a new place for her mother and I.

We're both struggling {financially}. It's expensive in La Joya and we both work {which means} there's a lot of challenges financially.

So her mom is like, 'Well, I don't talk to the kids about financial difficulties. I need to be strong for them. I don't let them know that I'm down. I need to be a rock for them and be solid and be strong for them.'

I didn't say anything to that, but I'm the opposite. If I'm worried about money or sad or happy, I share those feelings with my kids because I want them to know how important it is.

In the work we do {as parents}, it's important to be connected to your feelings. I want to model that for my children. {I want them to} know it's okay to be connected to your heart and to your feelings in a way that you can express them and feel them.

My son is naturally that way. My daughter Savannah is not. She's very cerebral. So when I tell you she's organized and a planner, you know she's definitely more in her head {while} my son is naturally more in his heart.

Definitely I like to talk about feelings {with my kids}. Sometimes, especially if something is brewing, I'll actually sit down with Savannah and we'll talk.

I actually intentionally will take time to take her aside and, you know, kind of dig deep, as deep as is comfortable for her. I'll say,

'Hey, I want to talk to you,' and we'll go somewhere and sit and talk.

She'll be like, 'Oh, man, here we go.' But she's okay with it. She doesn't fear it. She knows I'm going to talk about something that's probably going to be a little uncomfortable for her, for me.

She embraces it and she'll go with it until she starts to really not want to talk about it anymore. Then she'll let me know [and] I'll usually just say, 'Okay, we're good.' And I'm done.

So yeah, we talk about feelings."

Mark, forty-four year old Navy pilot, father of a fifteen year old daughter and an eleven year old son (divorced when his daughter was seven but stayed involved as a dad)

Sure I've Talked With My Daughter—About The Kind Of Dad I Want To Be

"Meaningful talks [with my daughter? They've been] short, not long. But yeah, I think we've talked about serious stuff before.

I talked to her about my temper and hers. I've apologized to her about how I've acted. I've talked to her about the type of dad I want to be for her, and the type of daughter I want her to be.

The talks [have been] more about behavior actually. We talked about her need to get on top of her behavior and be a good person.

We talked about our religion, and why it's important to me and why I want it to be important to her. That's the kind of stuff that pops up."

Ron, forty-seven year old school counselor and father of an eleven-year-old daughter and a twin eight-year-old daughter and son

We'll Even Talk About Her Menstrual Cycle If She Wants

My Daughter Knows I'm Accessible—Even Talking About Her Menstrual Cycle

"Yes. [Now that my daughter's a teenager] she's coming on strong with her menstrual cycle so there are physical changes that are coming earlier than I thought they would.

I wanted to show my daughters that I was comfortable, [even] talking to them about their menstrual cycle, talking about anything—that I am accessible and unconditionally loving."

Andrew, forty-six year old schoolteacher, father of two daughters age nine and ten

I Work Hard To Be A Good Dad—But It's Not Always Easy

To Overcome My Lack Of Connection—I Took My Daughter To Nice Restaurants

"She was very close with her mom at the time. I was working more and I pretty much kind of turned into my dad as far as [not being emotionally involved with the kids].

I mean, we did things together, on camping trips and whatnot. But the day-to-day life was more of—we were just in the same house. There weren't a lot of deep conversations or closeness in that regard, with her and I during that period.

> For many dads, being interactive took a lot of effort.
>
> Family outings were easy.
>
> It was being there one-on-one with your daughter and actually listening that took extra effort.

[To help overcome that] I'd deliberately take my daughter out to a nice restaurant. We would both dress up and do things in a classy way. [I'd] say, 'This is how a man treats a woman.' I deliberately chose to make that decision because I wanted to show her how valuable she was and how she should be treated, so she wouldn't settle for anything less.

I wasn't entirely comfortable with it because I hadn't tried this before. So I was, kind of—I know it's the right thing to do because I've read it. But I haven't seen it by example and I've never done it before myself.

It was early on when I was starting this, but it seemed to make sense. It was a good idea so let's give it a whirl. Then, when we would actually have the conversations about it after we've been doing that, she was grateful and in agreement, [basically saying], 'That was a good thing to do, dad.' "

Richard, fifty year old male nurse anesthesiologist, father of a twenty-five year old daughter and two sons

I'm Not As Tough A Dad As I Pretend To Be

"I'm not a tough enough dad to put the limits on [my daughter] that I probably should be. I love to portray myself as a super tough dad, but I'm not that tough."

Ron, forty-seven year old father of an eleven-year-old daughter and twin eight-year-old daughter and son

I Was Not Present For My Daughter Because I Also Was Not Really Grown Up Yet

"[I was] not present in her adolescence. Absolutely, being too wrapped up into my own stuff because I wasn't grown up then either."

George, seventy-five year old father of fifty-two year old daughter and two sons; also later became stepfather of another daughter (when she was a teenager) and a stepson

It's Been Difficult For Me To Connect Emotionally With My Daughter

It's A Constant Battle—To Not Be Isolated From My Kids Like My Father Was

"I think I'm very approachable {as a dad. But} the fact that I tend to isolate myself, the fact that I am not as natural with kids and my wife is, the fact that my wife will engage with them all the time, and that I have a lot of other interesting things I'd rather do, may make it appear to them at times that I'm not approachable, and I'll own that one.

And that's painful to own.

{He laughs} But you know—oh my god—the scary part also is that I've worked incredibly hard not to be my father. {But} it's so hard not to be. I just do {what he did} in a different way.

{I think} I'm so much more approachable and engaged than my father was. But my father was isolated and I kinda do that at times too. It's like a constant battle {for me} not to."

Ron, forty-seven year old school counselor and father of an eleven-year-old daughter and a twin eight-year-old daughter and son

I Was An Involved Dad— But I Never Had Deep Discussions With My Daughters

"I did a lot of sports with my kids. My kids are very good athletes so I played tennis a couple times a week with my kids. I had dinner with my kids, like dinner with {my stepdaughter} Laurie.

But one of the issues which I didn't have was, I didn't spend a lot of time alone with either one of my daughters. I spent a lot of time {with all of us} together, but...

Laurie and I would play tennis together, we'd run together, we'd do homework together. We did the whole 'everything' together.

I mean, I was very involved in their lives growing up [but not so much with the individual discussions]."

Len, sixty-eight year old attorney, father of a thirty-five year old son, a thirty-four year old daughter and a twenty-eight year old stepdaughter

Interaction With My Daughter Is Difficult—She Listens But Doesn't Give Feedback

"[My daughter is] not a real big talker back to me. She opens up I think, and talks a lot more with her mom [but] not with me.

I'll open and share with her, but it's more like she's kind of listening as opposed to giving me much feedback.

Most difficult for me is one of two things—it's either staying calm when my buttons start getting pushed, or accepting her for who she is rather than who I want her to be."

Ron, forty-seven year old school counselor and father of an eleven-year-old daughter and a twin eight-year-old daughter and son

My Daughter Is Noticing That I'm Much Easier To Be With Now

I Felt Disrespected Until I Realized—I Had A Large Part In What Was Happening

"[When my daughter disagreed with me] I felt disrespected and it made me angry.

I remember we were at a get-together for Christmas and there was something that I was saying [that] was annoying to her. So in front of everyone else she said something to me. I don't remem-

> For some dads, the secret to self improvement was learning to *not* react so strongly when their buttons got pushed.
>
> This was a difficult skill for many dads to develop.

ber exactly what it was, but it was like, 'Oh come on dad, knock it off.'

I remember feeling disrespected, so I stopped right there and said to her, 'Honey, I think that was disrespectful and I don't appreciate it at all.'

It was a really ugly and tense moment because you're in the presence of a bunch of other people and it's obvious this is not a happy discussion. It's just like an altercation.

Not that there was anything physical about it, but the words and the feelings were right out there and strong. [Then] there's that pregnant silence afterwards, 'What do we do with this?'

I was going through a million things in my head like, do I stand my ground on this one or just swallow it *again*? I'm conscious of the fact that [when] you swallow it, it's not a good idea because it blows your guts out. So do I express it?

In retrospect, when I look back on that situation and where I was at the time, a lot of it was my own issues and my own projection of the situation. It was not anything that she probably intended.

[Despite my reaction], she kind of stood her ground and like, 'Well, get over it, dad.' I mean, not directly that way, but it was— she didn't take it on and get all weepy and beat up by it. She was kind of like, 'Oh I don't know what that was all about but it's yours and not mine, dad.'

But that was definitely a time where there was a conflict.

[The problem I have is] I sometimes say the wrong thing and I get misunderstood. The story is, people don't hear me for who I am. I say something and they don't hear what I mean, they hear what I say. I'm misunderstood and they think I'm something that I know I'm not. So that's [why I said], 'Here we go again.'

[The good news is, this has not shown up] so much in the last several months because there's been some significant shifts. I'm more conscious of what's mine, [conflicts that I myself caused or imagined that may not actually be there].

[The reason for the change is] I've been very proactive at being able to grab those guys [in my men's group], and do 'conflict ownership' work or whatever they call it. That's when you go toe-to-toe with the other guy [where] he's the mirror and reflects back [your own emotion] to you. That kind of work has helped me discern, 'Okay, this [emotion] is something that's mine and has nothing to do with her.'

Being able to ferret out those details makes it easier to bypass anything that comes up [now with her] because most of the time it is [in my head and has nothing to do with her].

[Even she has noticed the change in me. She says], 'I'm glad to see you smiling dad {he laughs}. Glad to have you back.' Not in those words exactly but [she has noticed the change]."

Richard, fifty year old male nurse anesthesiologist, father of a twenty-five year old daughter and two sons

I Love Being A Dad To My Daughter

The Road Trips I Took With My Daughter Were Really Special

"[I remember] the trips we did. We circumvented Lake Superior one year, just she and I. We did camping and discovering new things. Yeah, we took a lot of car trips.

I remember when she was seventeen, she was a junior in high school and was trying to figure out what college she was going to apply to. She and a friend of hers and I took a trip down south to like, West Virginia and Virginia and up through New York and down through the Great Lakes and back home. It must have been two-thousand miles. That trip was just something really special—that she would want to do that with me. I've got lots of memories… yeah."

Lucas, fifty year old kindergarten teacher, father of a twenty-five year old daughter (divorced when his daughter was four but stayed one-hundred percent involved throughout her entire life)

Yes… My Daughter Knows How To Play Me Like A Violin

"I have a girly-girl. If I allowed her to, my daughter would shop every single day of the year. She never has enough clothes. She never has enough shoes.

She's a girly-girl, so she gets into her diva mode. I have to put her on an allowance of how much she can spend because she thinks, because she needs a lot of things, {he laughs}—needs, not wants—she needs these things.

And my daughter, she knows {how to} play me like a violin. She's like. 'But daddy will do it,' and she'll come sit on my lap and explain to me why she needs these certain things. 'But Daddy, I really need this.'

Yeah, she can play me. She knows that very well."

Darryl, forty-seven year old executive, father of seventeen year old son and fourteen year old daughter

My Daughter Doesn't Realize How Great She Is

"Yeah, I have lots and lots of memories. {I remember} watching my daughter on stage {at school}. She played Othello. She wasn't Othello, she was Iago in high school. And my heart was just bursting because she was so good and she didn't even know it, and she doesn't know it. She was very humble."

Lucas, fifty year old father of a twenty-five year old daughter

Some Surprises from this Chapter

Dads with a Daughter Age Thirteen to Sixteen

- **Freedom and Alienation:** School, social life and puberty all seemed to conspire to drive a wedge between fathers and daughters during this period.

  Daughters were generally busy defining themselves as distinctly different from their parents, often seeking independence from watchful eyes.

  Dads with difficulty communicating found this period expanded the sense of isolation from his daughter, because she was less available than in previous years. Other dads, who had been close, often experienced a sense of sadness and loss at a daughter starting to have her own life.

- **Puberty... and Boys:** Along with puberty, a whole new level of complexity emerged for many dads during this period.

  From sex education in school to frank discussions in movies, on television and over the Internet, having an open dialog with a daughter was becoming uncomfortable for a large percentage of dads.

  And once dating began, dads often became judgmental and uneasy. Even those dads who interacted well with their daughters often privately felt concerned and uncomfortable.

- **The Good Father... A New Set of Complications:** In trying to be a good parent and do-the-right-thing, some dads inadvertently pushed their daughters away in an attempt to rein in their activities.

  Although there would often be a reconciliation as a daughter entered her twenties, some fathers and daughters could not get over the conflicts that arose during this period.

  The good news... many dads mellowed and became more approachable as they got older, helping to ease earlier strained relations.

Stage Seven: Age 16-18 – Driving

– Could I Have the Keys Please –

Defining Factor: She gets her driver's license and suddenly has independence. She doesn't need to depend on her parents to drive her places, so they may not always know where she is. This is the beginning of a new type of independence.

Give her the car keys
and suddenly
she has a newfound
sometimes frightening
independence.

In this chapter
for many dads this is a prelude
to his daughter moving out.

This may be the first time
he regularly has no idea
where she is.

Inside this Chapter

Observations from 101 Dads of Daughters

- My Daughter Started Having More Responsibility
- Learning How To Drive Meant My Daughter Was Growing Up
- I Suddenly Saw My Daughter Becoming A Woman

- She Was Spending More And More Time With Her Friends
- Then There Was... The Dating
- As A Divorced Dad—It Can Get A Little Complicated

My Daughter Started Having More Responsibility

Putting Their Names On Our Checkbook Taught Our Daughters Responsibility

"One of the things we did with all three of our girls was to have their name on our checkbook. So at sixteen-years-old, they could take our checkbook, go to the grocery store and write a check for the groceries. They sort of took that as a, 'Hey, this is cool. I can actually do this, to figure out what the balance is and all that kind of stuff.' It was a very good learning experience."

Carl, sixty-five year old father of forty, thirty-eight and thirty-six year old daughters

I Was So Proud Of My Daughter For Taking Initiative And Not Panicking

"For part of the home-schooling curriculum, the {kids} would have to travel to another city and teach the younger kids. They had a whole curriculum they would {need to} develop. Little projects {like} songs they would sing, art projects they would do with the kids. [Also] they were doing the 'character' teaching at the time—honesty, whatever. So there were a lot of tools that they would use for teaching the younger kids.

{I remember} just feeling proud of her, the way she handled herself. {One time} she travelled by herself to meet with another girl. They were going to this program, I think it was in Louisiana. {But suddenly they realized} they had gotten on the wrong plane. This was before you had to have all that ID to get on a plane, {he laughs} and so they ended up on the wrong plane.

The other girl kind of dissolved into, 'Oh my God. What are we going to do? How are we going to get there?' {But} my daughter just pulled it together and handled it. She called home and said, 'What do I do?' She didn't dissolve and break down.

Just the fact that she handled it so well, to be out of town in a strange place, in an airport. I looked at that and went, 'Yeah, that's my girl!' And the way she handled the teaching too. She just grabbed the bull by the horns and would easily develop the curriculum. She would take charge, but [not] in a bad way. She felt comfortable doing it.

She did so with grace and creativity, in the stuff she did. She was vibrant about doing it. She loved what she did and she was very good at what she did. I remember [thinking to myself], 'Wow, she's good, she's quality stuff.' "

Richard, fifty year old male nurse anesthesiologist, father of a twenty-five year old daughter and two sons

Learning How To Drive Meant My Daughter Was Growing Up

I Loved Teaching My Daughter How To Drive A Bike—Then A Car

"I taught my daughter how to ride a bicycle, [and later] how to drive a car.

Oh God. [I have] lots and lots and lots of memories.

> The teacher-student coaching relationship felt right at some deep primal level.

One that I particularly like and she doesn't is when I taught her how to ride a bicycle. She wanted me to hang on to the bicycle seat and I let it go, and she fell. [But] I picked her up and we did it again.

Even when she could ride, she wanted me to hang on and I had to let go of it. That was one [memory] I loved–I've got so many.

I loved teaching her how to drive a car in parking lots. You know, having her be really afraid and watching her finally get out into traffic and do so well. I was so proud of her."

Lucas, fifty year old father of a twenty-five year old daughter (divorced when his daughter was four but stayed one-hundred percent involved throughout her entire life)

But When She Learned To Drive—I Realized She Was Growing Up

[But deep down] I knew she was going away from me. The bike and the car, learning how to drive… and her first date…

It was like, 'Oh okay, let it go, let it go, let it go.' Or she would stay out all night at theater parties and stuff. It was like, 'Yeah, this is what I wanted, yeah {his voice trails off, almost in sadness}."

Lucas, fifty year old father of a twenty-five year old daughter

I Suddenly Saw My Daughter Becoming A Woman

I Would Definitely Have Been Too Shy To Ask A Girl Like My Daughter On A Date

"When [my daughter] Emma graduated high school she was five-foot-eight. She was taller than most of the boys.

She graduated valedictorian in her class, so she was smarter than all the boys in her class, and she's beautiful. If I was a guy [in her school] I would be scared to death to ask a girl like that on a date."

John, fifty-six year old schoolteacher, divorced father of eighteen year old daughter (divorced when his daughter was seven but remained close to her)

She Was Spending More And More Time With Her Friends

At Her Age My Daughter's Memories Are About Hanging With Her Friends

"Living in southern California, my daughter's recent memories in the last two summers have been about going to the beach and hanging out with her friends. I think that's what she would remember most."

Mark, forty-four year old Navy pilot, father of a fifteen year old daughter and an eleven year old son (divorced when his daughter was seven but stayed involved as a dad)

Then There Was... The Dating

When My Daughter Started Dating I Was Joy-Filled And Terrified

"[What was it like when my daughter started dating?] Well, I would say it was 'anxious anticipation.'

I definitely wanted her to date. [But] I was a boy, and I realized what guys were after—that the threat was there, that the pressure was going to be there, and hopefully that she had the courage to really be who she was. If she wanted to have sex, [I hoped] she would, you know, make sure that it was done safely and that she would feel honored and respected and [not pushed or forced into it].

So I think the first date represented her stepping into her sexuality for me [and that felt] joy-filled and scary.

I just wanted my daughter to have a really wonderful experience with somebody who loved her, that she felt loved, and that it was special—that she wasn't just some [sex object].

What I have come to realize is that, because she held herself in such high regard, the boys in her life had to do the same thing, because that's just the way it was [and that made me feel a little better]."

Lucas, fifty year old father of a twenty-five year old daughter (divorced when his daughter was four but stayed one-hundred percent involved throughout her entire life)

It Gave Us A Bit Of A Scare—The First Time She Stayed Out Really Late With A Boy

"My Daughter might remember a time in which a boy from Albuquerque came out and she went on a date with him.

Since it's about a two-hour drive between the two, his parents came along and stayed in the town that we lived in.

She was a great talker, loved boys and all that kind of thing, and end-ing up staying out rather late that night. His parents and we were rather worried when it was about one in the morning. I remember that one very well {he laughs} but everything turned out okay."

Carl, sixty-five year old father of forty, thirty-eight and thirty-six year old daughters
(divorced twenty years ago but stayed involved as their dad)

As A Divorced Dad It Can Get A Little Complicated

Because I'm Not Always There—I'm Not Really Sure If My Daughter Has A Boyfriend

"She did date. She had a guy that was a boyfriend. [But] I'm not really a part of that [because as a divorced dad I don't live in the same house with her mom and her].

My daughter doesn't really like to talk with me about dating or about the boys [in her life]. I've actually asked her, if I run into her at the beach and there are boys around, for her to introduce me because I'd like to know who they are.

So yeah, I guess she's dating. She had a guy she was kind of dat-ing, same age as her and stuff.

But now that she's in [a private Catholic] high school and a lot of her friends go to the public school in La Joya, she hasn't met anybody at her new school that I would consider [her actually] dating. So as far as I know she's not dating anybody."

I Sometimes Get Put In The Middle— Between Her Mom And Her

"[As a divorced dad] she would call me [sometimes] because she just couldn't stand being with her mom anymore. She wanted to come live with me full time. She'd tell me to call a lawyer, talk to the judge, and do whatever it takes to try and [get her to] live with me all the time.

Couple things about that. One is, that's not really logistically an option because when I work, I'm [often] out of town, like I am right now. That was one.

The other one was trying to teach her that she needs to learn how to work it out with her mother and figure out how to get along with her because that's a tool she's going to use [throughout her life]. She's going to have bosses she doesn't like, she's going to have professors at school that she doesn't like, roommates that she doesn't like, people she works with, you know. It's something for her to learn how to deal with.

So at times she's called me because she just needs to talk about it, to figure out how to work it out.

I try and give her tools on how to deal with her mother. I've got a therapist in place that she's been talking to, and she and [my ex-wife] have gone in and talked to her together.

So that's an example of when my daughter's needed me."

When My Daughter Gets Really Unhinged—It Is Hard To Bring Her Back Down

"The most difficult thing with her is—it's only been recently— she's a little bit stubborn. She gets something in her head, [and] even if she knows it's right or not, she just won't budge. So it's hard to break through that. She becomes a bit irrational. That's the hardest part.

[For example] she gets really anxious because she's got some big social event to go to, but for some reason she can't go. [Maybe] I won't let her go because she's got some other commitment or something.

So she just gets really focused on that and becomes irrational. Normally she's very grounded, but when she becomes ungrounded and her feet start leaving the ground, it's hard to bring her back down. That's the hardest part."

Mark, forty-four year old Navy pilot, father of a fifteen year old daughter and an eleven year old son (divorced when his daughter was seven but stayed involved as a dad)

Some Surprises from this Chapter

Dads with a Daughter Age Sixteen to Eighteen

- **Dad's Dilemma:** The mixed feelings so many dads experienced during this period as they observed a daughter growing into a young woman, was noteworthy.

  Pride at realizing his little girl could now take care of herself was often tempered with an understanding that she would soon be moving out and living on her own.

  Even that great joy so many dads felt in teaching a daughter how to drive a car, was often contrasted with a sadness that this might be the last time he would play mentor to her.

- **Fear and Loss:** Even worse, having a driver's license now meant she no longer needed mom or dad to get places.

  For many dads there was a sense of fear and helplessness at the possibility of what trouble she could get herself into. Many Dads commented at how they remembered their own behavior at that age, so a daughter's newfound freedom was a concern.

  But when asked to recall how they felt during this period, the over-riding sentiment was sadness, a feeling that everything was about to change in the relationship with their daughter, as she ventured further and further from him.

Stage Eight: Age 18-25 – Independence

– Ready or Not, Here I Go –

Defining Factor: She is beginning to be fully independent
of her parents.

Although she feels mature, certain crucial brain functions are still
being developed (it's why some kids race cars, text-message while
driving, etc).

This may be the first time she is responsible for her own financial
well-being. School may be over, her career may be beginning and
she may be in a permanent relationship.

She is likely engaged sexually, through marriage or otherwise. She may
also give birth to her first child or may be considering having kids.

Welcome to the age of
the incredible vanishing girl
as his daughter is becoming
more deeply involved
with love, college, career
and a life on her own.

In this chapter
although many dads are unsure
how to let his daughter know
that he will always be there for her,
many dads tell of their great joy
in being there at some time of need
for his daughter.

Wanting to feel that he is needed
seems to resonate
with many dads.

Inside this Chapter

Observations from 101 Dads of Daughters

- I'm Noticing Changes As My Daughter Is More Grown Up
- My Daughter Finally Being On Her Own—That's Quite An Issue
- Boys—Yes That's Been Complicated

- I Loved Being There When My Daughter Really Needed Someone
- I Supported Her Taking A Big Challenge—That Brought Us Closer
- I Wouldn't Interact Directly With Her As Much As Her Mom Did

- The Secret Is <u>Not</u> Telling My Daughter What To Do
- I Do Have Conversations With My Daughter
- Tough Subjects Sometimes Make Guys Want To Disappear
- Sometimes It's Difficult Talking To My Daughter About Relationships
- Of Course It Would Be A Lot Tougher As A Single Parent

I'm Noticing Changes As My Daughter Is More Grown Up

Now That My Daughter Is A Mommy I Feel Her True Potential Is Limited

"Right now she has two daughters. The rest of the family would like to see her finish up her music degree and [maybe] do some teaching or something like that. But so far she's been babysitting [her kids as their mommy], which doesn't seem to utilize all of her talents as much as they could be. So I think she struggles a little bit more at having things together [in her life].

She was secretary for the college choir as part of her college work and really did some incredible stuff. She guided one bus for New York City to the airport while the teacher was on the other bus stuck in traffic. She managed to get everything organized, so at the airport the choir got checked in and on the airplane and ready to fly even though they were late. You know, a very, very neat person, very much together, knows how to handle stuff.

She was born on Thanksgiving so she was one of the older kids in the class. I think that may have helped her as far as leadership is concerned. [So I feel bad that she doesn't get to use more of that leadership] role she got to use as a teenager."

Carl, sixty-five year old father of forty, thirty-eight and thirty-six year old daughters

I'm Starting To See Her Personality Change—Now That My Daughter's In College

"My daughter seems very intelligent but not very open. There's a bit of a critical edge to her. I think a lot of it is [because] she's very critical of herself. I'd like to see some softening around the edges. I do see her personality change when she's with her friends. She's very bubbly and happy when she's with her friends. [So maybe sometimes] she either goes into an overwhelm [mode] or—I'm not sure what. I have seen some of that tenderness now that she's off in college."

Arthur, fifty-nine year old father of eight kids, including six daughters ranging from fourteen to thirty-two

For A While—She Didn't Want To Bring A Child Into This Messed Up World

"She chose finally to have a child. But there was a period there, where she was absolutely committed to not bring a child into this world because the world was going to hell and the hand basket."

George, seventy-five year old father of fifty-two year old daughter and two sons; also later became stepfather of another daughter (when she was a teenager) and a stepson

My Daughter Finally Being On Her Own—That's Quite An Issue

At College My Daughter Has Her Own Room—But She Misses Someone To Talk To

"My daughter was freaking out because she had a room of her own in college. She had never slept in a room by herself. She always had one or two sisters in her room with her.

You would think she would be looking forward to [finally] having her own room, but she's had the complete reverse response reaction. She was like, 'I don't know if I like this. I have no one to talk to.'

So we've made a point, and I particularly have made a point of going up to [her] college as often as possible. It's only been a couple months but we've been up there four or five times already, just to give her a dose of family."

Arthur, fifty-nine year old father of eight kids, including six daughters ranging from age fourteen to thirty-two

It's A Dilemma—I Want Her To Finally Move Out But I Love Having Her Here

"My daughter's still living at home. I kind of feel, with both of my kids, that they should be on their own by now, and that's a big problem between us.

I'm constantly on them with, 'I'm only charging you X amount of dollars for rent. If you lived on your own it would be [more]. You're staying here so you can make enough money to support yourself. I can't support you for the rest of your life.' that type of thing. So that's a problem.

> A daughter finally moving out was a mixed blessing for many dads.
>
> On the one hand they felt it was time; on the other hand they missed having her around.

[But the] positive is, she lights up my life. She's like a spark plug. I'm always interested in what she's doing. She's always got her mind going, whether it's in the wrong direction or not, trying to make a buck, trying to meet people, networking.

She's just a go-getter. She'll go twenty-four hours a day. I really respect her and I admire her for it, even though sometimes it drives me crazy that she doesn't just step back and relax a little bit once in a while.

I think that far outweighs any of the other problems I have [with her]. I think [maybe] my kids are just slow bloomers, you know, with being able to support themselves. She's out of college [only] two years so I'm not that concerned yet {nervous laugh}.

She is a slob, and [that] drives us nuts. I know she drove two of her boyfriends crazy with how sloppy she was.

[But I have to be careful of that]—trying to get them on the right track to be self sufficient but not negatively impacting their lives [by constantly bringing up] their faults.

[Still], if they listen to fifty percent of what you say, it's best I think."

Denis, fifty-six year old accountant, father is a twenty-four year old daughter and a twenty-eight year old son

She's Getting Married In A Couple Of Days—That's Going To Be Tough

"[My daughter is getting married in a couple of days and] I'll be a puddle [of tears].

I mean, I feel honored. But there's just something about the hand-off that's a major step. [I guess] it's really a good kind of sad, I don't know. It's what I worked for, but yeah, it's going to be hard.

I mean, it was something I envisioned, praying for her husband before I ever met him. [Then] when he finally showed up, [I started] feeling kind of protective about—is *he* what she needs, and that kind of thing.

[For me I guess it's] a lot of questions about, 'How do you feel about giving her away; how do you feel about the man she's chosen to marry; and do you feel diminished in any way, now that you are cut out of the picture?'

I process through a lot of that. It's kind of like, I'm *not* going to be the number-one man in her life anymore. She's moving on and that's a big transition.

[So it's] very bitter-sweet. I know it's right and I've been thinking, 'Yeah, this is exactly the way it should be.' But I'm going to miss [her]."

Richard, fifty year old male nurse anesthesiologist, father of a twenty-five year old daughter and two sons

The Whole Issue Of Boys—Yes That's Been Complicated

First She Was In Love With One Guy—Then It Was Another Guy—Then...

"I can totally see why my daughter fell in love with him. He never treated her badly—but he just wasn't interested in her the way she was interested in him. He was honest with her, so I don't have any negative opinions towards him. I really like him. He'll come by and say hi when he's in the area. So yeah, I felt awfully bad for her, but I don't blame him at all.

I think she's not [involved with anyone] right now although she's gone through several. In college, she fell in love with this guy—there's a whole Jewish thing here too by the way. My first wife was Jewish. I'm not and [my current wife] is not. But the kids, because their mother is Jewish, consider themselves Jewish, even if they don't go to temple or anything. But they consider themselves culturally Jewish. And their grandparents in Berkeley were Jewish, so they've got this whole thing where they see themselves as Jewish.

So she had this wonderful Jewish guy she went to school with, and fell in love with him. But then in her junior year she went to Mexico for an art thing—she's an artist. And she fell in love with this hot Latin guy, this Mexican guy who couldn't speak English, extremely handsome and very charming.

So she broke up with the guy from school, and then she spent a year in Mexico. Then she came back here and tried to keep this long-distance relationship going. He couldn't get a Visa to come here so she broke up with him.

[Since then] she's gone out with guys but she hasn't really fallen in love with anybody yet. She's a very attractive girl and gets lots of attention from guys [so I'm sure this won't be the end of it]."

Charlie, fifty-ish father of a twenty-seven year old son and twenty-five year old daughter Nadja (his wife died in a car accident when the kids were young. He's always been close to his kids)

I Wanted To Throw Him Out Because He Didn't Treat My Daughter With Respect

"I only remember this one guy that she dated and when she was in college. I was ready to throw him out of the house actually. I thought he treated her without respect."

George, seventy-five year old father of fifty-two year old daughter and two sons; also later became stepfather of another daughter (when she was a teenager) and a stepson

I Loved Being There—When My Daughter Really Needed Someone

It Made Me Feel Loved—She Called *Me* When She Was Scared

"[My daughter Lea recently] moved up to Portland, Oregon to go to Pacific Northwest College of Art. She had gone up this summer to try to find a place to rent with a friend. They hadn't found anything so she'd gone back [home] to Tucson. Then they found some place on Craigslist and arranged to rent it online without having seen the place or met the people, other than seeing some pictures.

> Almost all dads commented at how great it felt to be needed by their daughter.
>
> Coming to her rescue made them feel loved.

She got up there on a Friday night. They were renting a room in a house for a month while they were going to be looking for a better place for themselves. But it turned out that—Lea's description was, the woman who apparently was renting out the place was probably a meth addict. And her boyfriend appeared to have active tracks on his arms. So they got a very scary feeling about the place.

Unfortunately, they had moved in before they kind-of put their heads together and figured out that, 'It might not be good for us to be here at all.' And they'd [already] paid. They'd given her a check.

So Lea called me that night. [She and her friend] had driven away from the place and actually had put some of their stuff back in the car. She was really afraid, didn't know what to do, and felt like they shouldn't be there.

Could she stop payment on the check? What were her options? How should she do this? Should they go back and get a bicycle [they had forgotten]?

She was afraid [these people] might sell their stuff if my daughter and her friend weren't [back at the room] at night. Should they go back there and stay for the night? {He laughs}

So she called *me* because she was afraid of what her mom would do just because of her being in this situation. Kind-of, 'How could you let yourself get into this kind of a crazy situation,' rather than, 'Okay what can we do to get you out of this safely?'

It was really gratifying [that she called me]. It warmed my heart. I felt trusted and loved. At some level, I feel proud that I've been there for her in a way that she's not afraid to call and tell me the weird stuff that she's gotten into."

> *Carl, fifty-nine year old M.D. and director of an international non-profit organization, father of a twenty-one year old daughter (divorced when his daughter was four but stayed involved as a dad)*

When She Got Her Job She'd Call Me Every Day—I Felt Really Close To Her

"That was my daughter's dream from when she was in high school—to move to Denver and get a job with Snowboard Magazine, which she almost did but she didn't. [I mean], she was an apprentice there but never got hired as a full-time person.

We used to talk every day, 'What would you do Dad? I don't know if I'm doing the right thing. What do you think about this?' I don't know if it was the distance thing or what, but she would call me every day. I felt very close to her then.

I felt sorry for her too because she got herself into a situation where — I mean she wanted to be out there but it was just too much. All the things at the same time, trying to support herself, with the economy and all of that.

[But yeah], she used to call me all the time."

Denis, fifty-six year old accountant, father is a twenty-four year old daughter and twenty-eight year old son

I Was There For My Daughter When Her Relationship Went Through Ebbs and Flows

"I think when she's had difficulty [she would call me].

She grew to love this young man in high school. They were together for four or five or six years. [But] their relationship went through ebbs and flows. I think she needed me then to help her know what to do, or just for me to be there with her, yeah."

Lucas, fifty year old father of a twenty-five year old daughter (divorced when his daughter was four but stayed one-hundred percent involved throughout her entire life)

She Called Me When Her Mom Was Not Available—I Felt Very Close To Her

"I remember one time where she needed to talk. Something had come up in her life and she had called her mom who was working. She tried to talk to her mom but her mom got a phone call from one of her friends and cut her off. So she ended up talking with me.

That really set a tone for how things were going. She really unloaded on me a few times. I felt good. I felt very close to her."

Carl, fifty-nine year old father of a twenty-one year old daughter (divorced when his daughter was four but stayed involved as a dad)

I Supported Her Taking A Big Challenge—That Brought Us Closer

Her Adventure In Africa Brought Us Closer As a Family

"The relationship really started to solidify as [my stepdaughter] Tiffany got older, particularly her senior year in high school.

She's very smart, but she didn't do particularly well in high school. Mainly she just blew it off a lot of the times. She's very social, but what she [really] wanted was to go off and work as a volunteer in Africa, to work with kids.

> Several dads told us that supporting his daughter gave her confidence.
>
> Not so much financial as moral support... showing that you believed in her.

Actually, she's always had an interest in Africa. She has a huge heart, and I had gone to staff a [men's-work] weekend in South Africa [which may have given her some ideas].

We looked at the Peace Corps and things like that. We even went to a couple of Peace Corps information sessions, but they really don't like to take young people fresh out of high school. [They want] people with some college experience or some life experience.

So Tiffany did some research and she found another organization, called Humana People-to-People that actually sponsored volunteer activities—a lot in Africa but also in other parts of the world as well.

They have a training school out in northern California so Tiffany and I drove out there during spring break of her senior year. We basically visited there and met with the people and that.

It was just Tiffany and I. That was a real bonding experience for us, and helped us get closer together. That continued as she eventually enrolled in their program.

[She] spent six months out there training and doing fundraising, and then ended up going to Africa, Zambia, for eight months. During that whole process it was just a personal connection that she and I had. I mean, she would talk—and still does today—more frequently and more openly I think even then she does with her mother.

[Her mom and I] were in Colorado and she was in California, and [then] she was in Zambia. We talked by phone a lot. When she was overseas we talked [on the Internet] through Skype, probably at least several times a week during that whole period.

She was going through some challenges too. It was not easy when she first went to Africa, making that adjustment. [But ultimately] she had a great experience.

She was at an orphanage called Children's Town, which is about two hours outside of Lusaka, the capital of Zambia. There were three-hundred kids in the orphanage. Tiffany had personal responsibility for seventeen of those kids, with ages like, from ten up to seventeen.

She had them write letters to us. And when a cell phone tower was installed near Children's Town, she would occasionally put them on the phone to us and things like that.

It was wonderful. I mean, it really brought us together as a family, and it really solidified the relationship with Tiffany and myself.

Of course [there were times when I was worried for her], but you know, she turned out to handle it really well. I don't think I was as worried as her mother [that] basically she was on her own.

Tiffany would typically travel to Lusaka about every two weeks, which was about two hours away. There is no regular bus service.

Bus service is basically standing by the side of the road—which the roads are just old dirt roads—and people would come by with pickup trucks. You pay them money and you hop in the back of the pickup truck.

I remember at one point she's describing the situation there. She's in the back of the pickup truck and there's a mother and a baby and some goats. I mean, it's pretty far out."

Terry, sixty-two year old engineer and father of two sons age thirty-eight and thirty-four, a stepson age twenty-four and a twenty-one year old stepdaughter

I Wouldn't Interact Directly With Her As Much As Her Mom Did

I Didn't Talk Directly With My Daughter—I Supported From Behind The Scenes

"[When my daughter was going through this heartbreak with her boyfriend] most of it went on with her mom. She would call home and we'd talk, and then there was, uh… {his voice fades off}

I was working fairly steadily at the time and didn't have as much time off. I would buy a plane ticket for my wife, and she'd go out there and spend time with my daughter and, uh, help nurse her through that.

I was supportive from the background but we didn't talk a lot directly about it, she and I. It was more or less like my wife and I are one and we'd talk about it and then she talks to [my daughter] Jessica. That was more common than me having direct conversations with her about it."

Richard, fifty year old male nurse anesthesiologist, father of a twenty-five year old daughter and two sons

I Wish I'd Had More Direct Conversations—Rather Than Just Through Her Mom

"[If I could change one thing about my relationship with my daughter] I would say that would be more regular purposeful check-ins with her — 'How are we doing, what's going on in your life?'

I hear it [now] because she's currently living with us before she gets married, and so it's fairly available to me. But when she was away at college, that was largely done with her mom on the phone. I would just hear about it when they got off the phone.

So what I would change is to see that it's more direct rather than through mom. It would feel like I was more of a part of [her life] rather than an observer.

[I mean] I'm definitely a participant but it would be a shift towards being [even] more of a participant than an observer."

Richard, fifty year old male nurse anesthesiologist, father of a twenty-five year old daughter and two sons

The Secret Is Not Telling My Daughter What To Do

If I Were Stupid Enough To Tell My Daughter What To Do—She'd Do The Opposite

"[Now that she's] twenty-one, I don't have to tell my daughter what to do and what not to do. I'm real clear that it wouldn't be helpful, and the odds are she would do the opposite of what I said if I were stupid enough to tell her [what to do].

This is a trap many of these dads fell into: continually telling a daughter what to do.

The disconnect with a daughter could often be traced back to her not being trusted to figure things out for herself.

195

So when I have an opinion, I generally try to frame it in terms of experiences *I've* had which are somewhat similar [to what she's going through], and telling her about what happened with me… {he laughs} and then letting her do what she's gonna do."

Carl, fifty-nine year old M.D. and director of an international non-profit organization, father of a twenty-one year old daughter (divorced when his daughter was four but stayed involved as a dad)

I Do Have Conversations With My Daughter

Complaining To My Daughter About My Ex-Wife Is Not The Best Thing

"[Mistake I've made with my daughter?]

Complaining too much to her about her mom [my ex-wife].

I would like to share all that with her, but my daughter's relationship with her mother is very important to her and I should let that grow."

Carl, sixty-five year old ex-music teacher, with forty, thirty-eight and thirty-six year old daughters (divorced twenty years ago but stayed involved as their dad)

From Time-to-Time My Daughter And I Have A Really Wonderful Conversation

"My daughter and I don't talk all that much. Sometimes it's just an email and sometimes a phone call.

But three or four months ago she really opened up and told me a lot about her new job and some of her boyfriend stuff. She talks more to [my wife] about her boyfriend stuff [so it was a surprise that she was speaking to me about that].

She graduated in studio art and wants to go on to graduate school, so she's building up a portfolio, and she talked to me about that. Also, she's got a great job teaching ballroom dancing in San Francisco.

Both her grandparents have died in the last couple of years, and that's really been rough on her. [But] I think she's finally starting to come out of that and her life is really coming together now.

So we had a wonderful, wonderful, hour-and-a-half conversation. It doesn't happen a lot but, you know, it happens from time to time."

Charlie, fifty-ish father of a twenty-seven year old son and twenty-five year old daughter Nadja (his wife died in a car accident when the kids were young. He's always been close to his kids)

Sometimes It's Difficult Talking To My Daughter About Relationships

It's Easier Talking To My Son Than My Daughter—Guys Like To Disappear

"The big thing recently was my daughter decided she was going to break up with her boyfriend who she was living with. I spent a lot of time on the phone with her around that, around the whole disengagement process, and it was good.

I mean, quite frankly, it sort of fed my yearning to interact with her, my want to interact more with her, particularly as she gets older. I'm sure it fed that part of me that wants to be valued as a father, that wants to be a counselor to her, supportive of her and listen to her.

Still, it's more difficult for me to talk with her about relationships. Somehow it's a little bit easier when I talk to my son about relationships. Me being a male, him being a male, there's something a little bit easier to do that.

I can't even put my finger on it, but there are times when I say, 'Yeah, that's the way men are. They like to disappear {he laughs}. They don't like closure. They don't like to say they don't want to go out with you anymore. They like to just never call you again.'

I think it's a little bit more challenging there [the way guys are different than females]."

David, sixty-three year old real estate appraiser and Vietnam vet, father of a thirty-seven year old son and a twenty-nine year old daughter (divorced when his daughter was eight but stayed very engaged with his children growing up)

Of Course It Would Be A Lot Tougher As A Single Parent

Even Though My Wife And I Are Divorced—I'm Glad I'm Not A Single Parent

"Sometimes it felt like I was a single parent. So I'm sort of thankful now that her mom was able to take care of a few more of the things, because it'd be tough for me to do it all [by myself].

[It's finally] alright now, at this point in time. Every once in a while I have to [remind] myself of that {he laughs}."

Carl, sixty-five year old father of forty, thirty-eight and thirty-six year old daughters (divorced twenty years ago but stayed involved as their dad)

Some Surprises from this Chapter

Fathers with a Daughter Age Eighteen to Twenty-Five

- **Silent Sadness:** Surprisingly, even dads who struggled through a troubled relationship with their daughter commented at how this period, where she moved out, to college, to a life on her own or to marriage, was emotionally difficult for them.

  Sadness was sometimes coupled with a frustration that they would no longer be able to rescue her, especially from a bad relationship.

- **Needing to Be Needed:** Perhaps the most universal trait emerging from these dads was a sense of joy whenever a daughter truly needed them... except dads who could not help financially found their inability painful.

  However, if she was scared, had relationship problems or just needed support over a difficult issue in her life, dads almost universally commented on how great they felt at *"being there for her."*

  Predictably, this joy was amplified for many when a daughter would go to dad instead of mom for help or support over an issue.

- **The Power of a Dad's Support:** A dad's support was surprisingly crucial for some daughters' willingness to accept an ambitious or complex challenge in their life.

- **On Her Becoming a Mommy:** For daughters who gave birth during this period, although most dads enjoyed being a grandfather, almost all reminisced with a degree of sadness at how, *"my little girl is all grown up."*

Stage Nine: Age 25-49 – Distance

– The Long and Winding Road –

Defining Factor: Generally she has moved out and is living on her own, by herself or with someone she may love—married or cohabitating, or living with friends.

She may be at the beginning of her career or profession.

If she does not live nearby, interaction may be only during the holidays and vacation if at all. Otherwise, interaction with her is by phone, text messaging and the Internet. She may have children, with dad now being a grandfather.

She's gone, living her own life.
So dad is unable to rescue his daughter
from bad relationships.

But he can be there for her
if she needs someone
to talk things out.

In this chapter, many dads
get a real charge
when he's able to be there
to help or rescue his daughter.

Despite the distance,
for some dads
the relationship with his daughter
is getting stronger.
For others, it is not.

Inside this Chapter

Observations from 101 Dads of Daughters

- My Daughter Now Has A Life Of Her Own
- Our Interaction Has Changed Now That My Daughter Is Older
- I Share My Feelings And Expectations With My Daughter

- I Was There For My Daughter When She Really Needed Someone
- As I Went Through Changes In My Life—That Affected My Kids
- It's Great Spending Quality Time With My Daughter

My Daughter Now Has A Life Of Her Own

It's Gratifying Seeing Your Daughter Stand On Her Own Two Feet

"Ultimately daughters become their own person. They don't need you anymore and that's okay. It's really okay.

As a matter of fact, you should look forward to it—that they are standing on their own two feet, with a life of their own, and dreams and goals of their own. It's quite gratifying."

Arthur, fifty-nine year old father of eight kids, in luding six daughters ranging from age fourteen to thirty-two

My Daughter Enjoys Life—And Her Husband Is Absolutely Great

"She has a beautiful relationship with her two daughters and her husband. I think [my daughter has an] enjoyment of life about where she's at, who she is, what she could do with herself.

She's a very successful lady. And she says she's very capable of handling anything that comes her way. I feel quite solid about her.

As far as her husband—you know, when it comes down to my three sons-in-law, I think the three sons-in-law that I have are just absolutely great men. I have a great deal of respect for them. I've had experiences of talking with them in a very good positive way."

Carl, sixty-five year old father of thirty-eight and thirty-six year old daughters (divorced twenty years ago but stayed involved as their dad)

Our Interaction Has Changed Now That My Daughter Is Older

I Wish I Heard From My Daughters More Often—I Wish They Lived Closer

"I'm looking very much forward to retirement in about two-hundred days. I'm hoping I can get up to Seattle and spend a couple of weeks with [my daughter and her family].

I would like to hear from her more—that's true of all three of my kids. I'd like to be [geographically] closer to them. That's frustrating.

Some dads expressed sadness at *not* being able to spend time with their adult daughter.

Others have found the connection has increased with age, aided by telephone and the Internet.

I am closest to [my daughter] Jennifer because she lives closer [than the others], only about a hundred miles away. Still, the distance [is definitely most difficult]. I'd like to be with her more.

[Also] I'm working too much right now [and that limits the time I could spend with her]. I work seven days a week so I don't have as much time for them as I would like to have.

[And besides] the time problem, she's getting quite close to her mom and I'm jealous.

[So yes], I would like to be a bigger part of her family, but sometimes it's difficult. It's not a major thing but it is something that comes up once in awhile."

Carl, sixty-five year old ex-music teacher, with forty, thirty-eight and thirty-six year old daughters (divorced twenty years ago but stayed involved as their dad)

My Daughter And I Talk More Now Than When She Was Younger

"So now my daughter's remarried. She married a guy that's real good to her and real supportive, and she's much happier.

I don't know that we did a whole lot of deep talking when she was a younger girl. But now she'll call me up and talk to me about what's going on with her life, and share with me what's going on with her ex-husband and her children.

She has a younger son by her first husband. She's trying to be a mother to a rebellious son, and her daughter seems to be back and forth with that [so we'll talk about that].

At times we're closer and at other times we're not as close, because she's afraid of how the information may impact me and how I will respond. She knows I'm very protective of her and so, sometimes she's guarded with what she tells me."

Donnie, fifty-six year old father of a thirty-two year old daughter and thirty year old son (divorced when his daughter was eight but remained close to her)

I've Been Able To Spend More Time With My Stepdaughter Now That She's Older

"As [my stepdaughter Jamie] has gotten older, I've spent more time with her than probably any of my [other children]. My son has been away in New York since he was eighteen, I guess. [And my daughter's] been married for six years now. [So I have more time for Jamie]."

Len, sixty-eight year old attorney, father of a thirty-five year old son, a thirty-four year old daughter and a twenty-eight year old stepdaughter

I Share My Feelings And Expectations With My Daughter

My Daughter Calls Me Just To Find Out How My Day Is Going

"I share with my daughter what my relationship is like with my present fiancée, and the difficulties I'm having with work or coping with what it's like being a future stepfather dealing with my future stepkids.

I think that my daughter and I have a real good line of communication in that way, yeah.

I call her probably a number of times during the week. I'll call her and tell her I love her, and leave messages on her voicemail. She called today just to find out how my day was going."

Donnie, fifty-six year old father of a thirty-two year old daughter and thirty year old son (divorced when his daughter was eight but remained close to her)

I Tell Her My Expectations—My Daughter Can Take It Or Not

"I'm pretty cool now about telling [my daughter] what my expectations are. That doesn't mean they're necessarily her expectations. Those are my thoughts.

I don't have an issue giving any of my kids what my thoughts are. Whether they take it and like it, that's their problem. I'm not so worried about it. They can do what they want with it."

Len, sixty-eight year old attorney, father of a thirty-five year old son, a thirty-four year old daughter and a twenty-eight year old stepdaughter

I Was There For My Daughter When She Really Needed Someone

My Daughter And I Spoke Often When She Was Considering Her Divorce

"[We spoke a lot] when my daughter was thinking about getting her divorce, and what her life was like living with her first husband. We did a lot of talking about that."

Donnie, fifty-six year old father of a thirty-two year old daughter and thirty year old son (divorced when his daughter was eight but remained close to her)

A highpoint for many of these dads was being a lifeline for a daughter in her moment of need.

Through a daughter's divorce, death of her spouse, alcohol and drug addiction, a father's dedication to his daughter was often a defining factor in her coping with and recovering from a dire situation.

I Was There For My Daughter When Her Husband Died

"My daughter needed me when her husband died. Probably [important that I was there for her] when [her husband] Jimmy died in our adult lives."

George, seventy-five year old father of fifty-two year old daughter and two sons; also later became stepfather of another daughter (when she was a teenager) and a stepson

My Daughter Conquered Her Alcoholism—In Part Because We Stuck With Her

"[With my younger daughter, I'm comfortable] talking about growing up, working, school, the importance of life—name a subject—drinking.

Remember, my big kids were [grown up and] out of the house. Then I had an alcoholic [younger] daughter for how many years? For five or six years that I know of. And then [going through rehab with her]. So I spent the last seven years talking to her about life, about what it means [for me] not to be enabling and learning how to make her more self sufficient.

I didn't have to deal with my big kids at all with that kind of stuff. My big kids were always self-sufficient.

I think 'self-esteem' is the right word. I don't know how you teach that. We've done our best [but] I think you've got it or you get it. I don't know if you can teach someone to have self-esteem.

[I think it helped that as a father my daughter got] some-body who didn't throw her out. [Instead she got] somebody that supported her and convinced her to become clean about drinking, about drugging. [She got somebody to help her] understand that she's going to have to live on her own and learn life and take care of herself—that I'm not [going to be] there all the time.

I Learned That I Can't Fix Everything—That's Been A Tough Lesson

The last six years I've spent learning what it means to be the father of an alcoholic daughter and what all those things mean. I put a lot of hours into that girl.

I learned limits, I guess that's what I learned.

I didn't have limits with [my older daughter] Laurie. Laurie didn't need limits. [But with my younger daughter] I learned how to do limits. I learned [that] 'limits' means you can do anything you want to [try to] fix it, but *you* can't fix it.

In my own mind I can fix everything. With my big kids I didn't have anything to fix so it didn't make much difference. But when you have a daughter that needs a lot of things to be fixed, you learn that, again, *you* can't fix them. *They* have to fix them.

That's been a really tough learning experience for me as a parent. I believed [if] I told Jamie to stop drinking, showed her why, clearly she'd stop drinking. [But I] found out alcoholism is a disease. I didn't even know that. So it's not something she really could just deal with. [And worse], I could actually enable her.

So that's a major league learning experience—took a long time to learn that.

I think most of us as parents believe we can fix most things [for our kids]. At least, I always thought that. Why should my kid have to suffer growing up? [I can] take care of that too.

Her Addiction Put Stress On The Family—But It Also Brought Us Closer

[Did it put stress on our family or did it bring us closer?] Absolutely both. Absolutely both.

It makes you closer, but there's a lot of heartache in that. I mean, this is serious, serious heartache when a child has alcoholism or diabetes or, God forbid, cancer or whatever disease you've got. So there's a lot of stress in that stuff.

{Laughing} I could have been close without that aggravation. But you got the cards you're dealt with. You don't have any choice in life.

Interesting enough, I don't think my big kids had to suffer. [It's only] the little one who has had to suffer a lot.

We were pretty honest about what was going on in our family. I mean, one thing we didn't do is hide stuff. We talk about lots of stuff. I'm not smart enough to remember what to hide. [So during the seven years of her recovery, my older kids were involved]. Absolutely. Absolutely. Clearly involved.

Physically they would come to certain events. [Otherwise] they knew when Jamie went to Hazelton [the addiction treatment center]. They always knew exactly where we were and the kinds of stuff that we were participating in. They knew that every Monday night you couldn't get us between, what is it, eight-thirty and eleven because we went to an Al-Anon meeting. There was nothing hidden about any of the stuff.

Today Her Life Is Finally Terrific—I Give Her Credit For That

I talk to Jamie almost every day, so there's not much that I haven't said to her or that I don't try to tell her every day.

I surely tell her I love her every day. I surely tell her things that I expect from her and what I would like to see happen. I'd like to clearly see her being more independent about her life. I talk to her about that.

Nothing's perfect, but is Jamie terrific today? Yeah!

I mean she's [always going to have to fight not falling back into it]. It's like, I relate it to someone who, if they said you can't have bread at any meal and it's offered to you every day, [that's always going to be tough for her].

But do I give her a lot of credit? Have I learned a lot through Jamie?

Probably I've learned as much through Jamie or more than I've learned through my big kids. I guess I've learned that her life is her life and I can't control much of it. She needs to fix herself. I can't fix her.

There's some real lessons in that stuff. They were very hard lessons."

Len, sixty-eight year old attorney, father of a thirty-five year old son, a thirty-four year old daughter and a twenty-eight year old stepdaughter

As I Went Through Changes In My Life—That Affected My Kids

After My Wife Died I Started Dating—My Kids Feared Our Relationship Would Suffer

"I dated after my wife died. Both Heather and her two brothers were sort of frightened that I would not continue their relationship much longer. They were very afraid but they wouldn't tell me anything."

George, seventy-five year old father of fifty-two year old daughter and two sons; also later became stepfather of another daughter (when she was a teenager) and a stepson

It's Great Spending Quality Time With My Daughter

Going On A Car Trip Or Having Dinner Together Helps Us Stay Close

"Last Christmas we took a trip from Los Alamos up to Washington State, and we spent a lot of time in the car. Other times she comes down here and we'll go out for dinner and all that kind of stuff. [That helps us stay connected]."

Carl, sixty-five year old father of forty, thirty-eight and thirty-six year old daughters (divorced twenty years ago but stayed involved as their dad)

Some Lessons from this Chapter

Fathers with a Daughter Age Twenty-Five to Forty Nine

- **Weakened and Strengthened Relationships:** It was surprising how different the reactions were from dads, now that a daughter was living away from home.

  For some it was a longing for a time when they were closer geographically and emotionally to their daughter, while others found the relationship with their daughter actually strengthened in these adult years.

  The dads who fared best tended to make time to regularly talk to their daughters, often through extensive phone or Internet conversations. One dad even scheduled a regular conference call with his kids, to keep them all in touch despite their distances apart.

  The better-connected dads also scheduled periodic vacations and family get-togethers where they could spend quality time with a daughter and perhaps her family, if she had one.

- **Open Dads Fared Better:** Not surprisingly, dads who were open about their feelings and were willing to share details about themselves and about life seemed closer to their daughters than those who did not.

- **Being There for Her:** A high point for many dads was being able to comfort a daughter if she had experienced a divorce, a death or some other hardship.

- **Tough Lesson:** One of the toughest lessons for many dads was observing a daughter with family or personal hardships, and realizing he could not fix everything for her.

Stage Ten: Age 49+ – Maturity

– Nothing More Important Than Family –

Defining Factor: She has a somewhat defined life, may be approaching menopause, may be searching for meaning in her life.

If she has children, they may be moving away from home, providing her more free time to reflect on her life. She may be calmer and more available than in previous decades.

Although many dads say,
"I am my daughter's biggest fan,"
few actually ever tell her,
"I'm Proud of You."

In this chapter,
time sometimes heals the wounds
between a father and his daughter.

Becoming a grandfather,
or having his daughter
become the caretaker for an aging father—
these add a new dimension to
the father-daughter relationship.

But regardless of his situation
or the relationship with his daughter,
a surprising number of the older dads confide,
"In the end,
nothing is more important than family."

Inside this Chapter

Observations from 101 Dads of Daughters

- Now That I'm Older My Kids Have Gotten Closer To Me
- This Generation Is Not As Connected To Family As When I Was Young
- The Role Of "Dad" Is Different Today
- My Relationship With My Daughter Is Better Now That We're Older
- I'm My Daughter's Biggest Fan
- My Daughter Is Able To Confide In Me

- It's Difficult Knowing That My Daughter Is Struggling
- Because We Live So Far Apart—Our Relationships Suffer
- We Try To Stay Connected As A Family Despite The Distance
- Except For Babysitting—I'm Not That Important To My Daughter
- Now That I'm Older My Daughter Is My Caretaker

- Her Illness Has Brought Us closer—At My Age I Love Being Needed
- I Love Being A Grandfather
- In The End Nothing Is More Important Than Family

Now That I'm Older My Kids Have Gotten Closer To Me

My Relationship With My Daughter is Closer Today—Time is Running Out

"[My relationship with my daughter] is probably closer today than ever. [What has changed is my] age. My age has brought people closer to me because they figure, time is running out so they'd better take advantage of it. They don't say that, but I'm sure that's in their mind."

Walter, eighty-one year old retired businessman, father of a fifty-six year old daughter and three sons

This Generation is Not As Connected To Family As When I Was Young

When I Was Young We Used To Do Everything With Family—Not So Much Today

"It's great having a family, although I think now young peo-ple—even my own daughter and son—have [less a connection to family] than in my generation. Their biological family is not as important maybe as their friends and associates.

In my generation it was more—we did everything with the fam-ily, you know, the biological family. I come from an Italian back-ground and that was the norm. But I don't see that happening now as much."

Leonard, seventy-three year old ex- school music teacher, father of a forty-six year old son and a thirty-three year old daughter (divorced later in life but has stayed close to his daughter)

The Role Of "Dad" Is Different Today

Masculinity Today Is About Strength—But It's Also About Emotional Connection

"[The concept of 'masculinity' is different today than when I was young].

[Today it's about] being able to cry, having a sense of emotions, not being shut down, being powerful when the need for power is necessary and being loving—being able to hug and touch and that sort of thing. I don't mean sexually at all, but I mean being connected.

People of my era, because of the mostly Euro-centered cultures, didn't have that. Our parents were raised in a different environment.

[But] today I think daughters want a sense of emotional connections and a physical connection and strength. Masculinity [today] is strong but it's also loving."

Red, seventy-eight year old father of forty-nine year old daughter, three sons, three step sons and a fifty-year-old stepdaughter (his stepdaughter was eighteen when he came into her life)

I'm Not Sure If I Should Have Been More Father Than Friend To My Daughter

"Maybe I was being a dad without being a parent. I don't know. [Maybe] I need to find the two and differentiate. I was probably more friend than father [to my daughter]."

George, seventy-five year old father of fifty-two year old daughter and two sons; also later became stepfather of another daughter (when she was a teenager) and a stepson

I've Told My Kids Everything That Needs To Be Said

"In my stage of life, if I hadn't said it up to now, it's my problem, not theirs {he laughs}."

Red, seventy-eight year old father of forty-nine year old daughter, three sons, three step sons and a fifty-year-old stepdaughter (his stepdaughter was eighteen when he came into her life)

My Relationship With My Daughter Is Better Now That We're Older

I'm More Involved With My Daughter Today Than When She Was Growing Up

"[On a scale of one to ten, ten being best, how would I rate myself as her father?]

{Laughing} When? Now? So now [I'm] a ten. If you go back twenty years, I'd give you a TWO because I told you that I was a non-participant parent because I had no profession.

> Something about age seems to bring dads and daughters closer. Even some fathers who were estranged from their daughters for decades found a mellowing of the relationship later in life.

I'm an 'e-literate' guy. I was out on the streets hustling to make money to feed [my family] in comfort [so they could] live in a nice house and have a car at the door. That [stuff] doesn't fall from the sky. I had no time to do both. I'd leave on a Monday and come back on a Thursday. Next question!"

Walter, eighty-one year old retired businessman, father of a fifty-six year old daughter and three sons

We Talk To Each Other As Adults—Not Just As Father And Daughter

"[So on a scale of one to ten, with ten being best, how would I rate myself as Allison's dad]?

Nine out of ten. I've had all these experiences in life [with her], and I'm nearby geographically and nearby emotionally, and we can talk to each other as adults, not father and son or father and daughter. There's an adult aspect to our relationship. Yeah."

Red, seventy-eight year old father of forty-nine year old daughter, three sons, three step sons and a fifty-year-old stepdaughter (his stepdaughter was eighteen when he came into her life)

I'm More Approachable Now In My Second Marriage Than I Was In My
First

"The thing that has warmed my heart is, the relationship between
[my new wife] Jean and my daughter has become really open. I
think my daughter Heather has finally accepted Jean in a more
open way.

I think it's because my daughter has matured [so] she's more
inclined to let her feelings [out now].

Her mother and I never shared feelings, so my kids grew up in
a culture where we didn't talk [about] that stuff. [In a large part
that's] because I grew up in a culture where it was really big to
talk about that stuff. [As a child, those are the kinds of things]
that my mom hadn't talked about.

My daughter Heather and I do [talk about our feelings] now—
over the last ten years, because I've changed.

I'm a worrier {he laughs}. [But what] I've discovered is, that's
exactly what needs to happen in the relationship that I have with
[my new wife—that I can talk about the things that are worrying
me].

We're really far more connected emotionally and open than I was
with my first wife. Not that there wasn't tremendous love [in my
first marriage]. It's just, we didn't talk about things that bothered
us.

Am I more approachable [now]? Yeah. [Have I always been
approachable]? No."

*George, seventy-five year old father of fifty-two year old daughter and two sons; also later
became stepfather of another daughter (when she was a teenager) and a stepson*

My Daughter's Illness Has Brought Us Closer

"I think I've always been closer to my son [than my daughter]. However, this is changing now as they grow older.

I live physically closer to my daughter.

Also, she's developed an illness, multiple sclerosis, so that has bought us closer together."

Leonard, seventy-three year old ex- school music teacher, father of a forty-six year old son and a thirty-three year old daughter (divorced later in life but has stayed close to his daughter)

I'm My Daughter's Biggest Fan

I'm Proud Of How She's Taken Care Of Herself—Even Through Her Divorce

"I'm proud of my daughter, her strength.

She's a strong woman, she can handle herself. Example is she lives alone, she broke up with her husband and her kids, some went this way, some went that way.

But they all eventually came back because I guess they realize she was [there for them].

Many dads found it easier to tell *us* about how proud they were of their daughter, than to tell their own daughter.

For a reason that no dad could really explain, the words, "I'm proud of you," are often difficult to say later in life.

[But] she also went and got herself a new education. She went and got herself a new job. She's going forward with her life and that's hard to do. She's a fifty year old woman, don't forget."

Walter, eighty-one year old retired businessman, father of a fifty-six year old daughter and three sons

My Daughter's Doing Great Despite Having To Manage A Difficult Life

"I think the greatest thing that my daughter had done is to manage a very difficult life—with a difficult partner and a son who has required considerable medical attention because of his asthma and allergies.

But she's put it together. She's fought a good fight and she's still loving life to the extent that she can."

George, seventy-five year old father of fifty-two year old daughter and two sons; also later became stepfather of another daughter (when she was a teenager) and a stepson

My Daughter Is Able To Confide In Me

My Daughter Talks To Me About Her Insecurities—I Wish I Could Fix Them

"Oh yeah [I have pretty meaningful talks with my daughter. She talks to me] about her husband and her marriage and did he play around on her or didn't he, and that kind of stuff. I don't think he did, but who knows?

She has a degree of insecurity that I wish I could fix. But that's because of her childhood, you know. We all [have insecurity] to just some degree or another, let's face it."

Red, seventy-eight year old father of forty-nine year old daughter, three sons, three step sons and a fifty-year-old stepdaughter (his stepdaughter was eighteen when he came into her life)

When Her Husband Died—I Suddenly Felt More Connected To My Daughter

"At one point my daughter came to Chicago to visit me and invited me to lunch.

I remember the restaurant, you know, the whole thing about looking down at the plate and saying, 'Uh, there's something that I need to share with you... I'm pregnant.'

{He sighs} It was like, 'Okay. Tell me more about that.'

It turned out to be Jimmy, a young man [I had known]. So at least it was somebody that I knew. And it wasn't by accident, it was by intention.

So she [eventually] gave birth to my grandson. That was wonderful to have a grandson.

[Over the years] the relationship between her and Jimmy was not particularly good. He was too narcissistic I think, to have a good relationship with her.

So that was a struggle for a long time—until Jimmy died a couple of years ago. We believed it was a heart attack but we really don't know. They didn't do an autopsy.

She discovered him in his house because they lived about a mile apart. My grandson would go there on Wednesday afternoons, then on Saturdays. Unfortunately she couldn't raise Jimmy on the phone. So she went to check before she dropped her son off, and discovered Jimmy dead on the floor in his bedroom.

[That was] painful, very painful. I was more in pain for my grandson. He would have been, at that point probably thirteen, fourteen. He's eighteen now, so [it's been] less than four years now.

[But Jimmy's death] has opened up [my relationship with my daughter]. It's taken a kind of a burden and a thorn out of her paw. [Also, her relationship with Jimmy had been something] that I had a lot of judgments around. I kept wanting her to be more demanding of Jimmy, to request more support for their son. But she wouldn't do that [and] I've never quite understood it. And so, I had to let it go.

After Jimmy died we had a lot more conversations about where this [life] is gonna go, what's gonna happen. I felt more connected and more able to support her at that point.

[Still, many topics have remained off-limits] Her family is off limits. And we don't talk about what kind of a mother [my ex-wife] is except to acknowledge that she is doing a great job. And we don't talk about the relationship with her husband. None of my business.

[I've learned to not talk to any of] my kids about the relationships with their partners. That's their life and they've chosen it. If they want to ask me, 'What do you think,' I'm certainly willing to share what my thoughts are. But I don't intrude into their relationship."

George, seventy-five year old father of fifty-two year old daughter and two sons; also later became stepfather of another daughter (when she was a teenager) and a stepson

I Have To Be More Careful Talking To My Daughter Than To My Son

"I would say [my conversations with my daughter have not been] as deep and not as often as with my son, even to this date.

I have to be careful. Although she's very tolerant, a couple of times she told me, 'I [wouldn't] mind the things that you tell me if it were anybody else, but not my father.'

So I have to be a little careful and sensitive to things like that. With my son it's totally different."

Leonard, seventy-three year old father of a forty-six year old son and a thirty-three year old daughter (divorced later in life but has stayed close to his daughter)

It's Difficult Knowing That My Daughter Is Struggling

I Wish My Daughter Would Ask For More Of What *She* Wants

"The most difficult [thing] for me has been a longing that my daughter would be willing to really speak what's in her heart. It was a long period when she would do that [but she doesn't seem to anymore].

[What I mean is, I'd like her] to stake out her territory with people who are in her life. She's [too] willing to accept what [people are doing] and not demand the change. It's hard for me to see her do that.

She has so much to offer and she's a strong woman, but there comes a time when she will not take charge and just say, 'Hey, here's what I need and what I want, and I'd like you to give that to me.'

It's hard. I know she's struggling financially—the burden of being a single mom. She has done a magnificent job with her son."

George, seventy-five year old father of fifty-two year old daughter and two sons; also later became stepfather of another daughter (when she was a teenager) and a stepson

A painful topic among older dads was knowing a daughter was struggling financially, physically or emotionally and he could do nothing to help her.

Because We Live So Far Apart—Our Relationships Suffer

Being So Far Away It's Difficult For My Daughters To Maintain a Close Relationship

"[My daughters] see each other maybe twice a year. But because they're geographically eleven hundred miles apart, [having them maintain a close relationship] is pretty hard to nurture.

We've tried to nurture it because we're all family, and it's growing. But it's difficult because of the geography."

George, seventy-five year old father of fifty-two year old daughter and two sons; also later became stepfather of another daughter (when she was a teenager) and a stepson

We Try To Stay Connected As A Family Despite The Distance

We All Get On A Conference Call Sunday Evenings—And Enjoy Holidays Together

"[Even though my family is scattered geographically], we all get on the call using Skype [the Internet conference-call service. Skype lets us get together as a family and] talk at least once a week.

Actually, unless one of us is occupied, [we all] hit the clock fairly regularly on Sunday nights. Me and two or all-three of my kids get on Skype and have a conversation for about an hour and a half.

We try very hard to [keep it regular].

Sometimes, one of them doesn't make it because of a conflict or if there's homework to do for one of their kids. But pretty much [my daughter] Heather is there, and I'm there. Then typically she and I talk at least once more during the week.

Also, for many, many years [around Thanksgiving, my daughter] Jean and I would pack our bags and jump on the plane Sunday morning before Thanksgiving, go to New York and spend Sunday, Monday, Tuesday and Wednesday morning doing theater and museums.

Then Heather and my grandson Andrew would come in the city. We would do a matinee and dinner at our favorite restaurant, and then go to her house for Thanksgiving, or we'd go to my son's place in Connecticut.

So that was the Thanksgiving routine for a long time."

George, seventy-five year old father of fifty-two year old daughter and two sons; also later became stepfather of another daughter (when she was a teenager) and a stepson

Except For Babysitting—I'm Not That Important To My Daughter

My Daughter Has So Many Friends—I Wish I'd Been More Like Her

"My daughter probably would say that I'm a good grandfather and I'm available to help out whenever she needs somebody to stay with the kids.

{He lowers his voice} …but my daughter would not consider me that important, except for babysitting. I don't think she would describe her relationship with me as the most important [compared with] probably her peers, her husband, her colleagues.

I'm happy that, unlike me, she has lots of friends.

It makes me very happy that she enjoys the work she does, and that she has the social contacts that I didn't have. She has so many activities and so many friends.

Her calendar is full, mine is empty. I don't have as many friends as she does so I admire that in her. I think that's probably the way I would have liked to be.

I like being invited to be with her and her friends. I enjoy meeting her friends and her when I'm allowed, when I'm invited. And this is often enough. So yeah, that's what I enjoy the most."

Leonard, seventy-three year old ex- school music teacher, father of a forty-six year old son and a thirty-three year old daughter (divorced later in life but has stayed close to his daughter)

Now That I'm Older My Daughter Is My Caretaker

My Daughter Is My Advisor—I Trust Her Judgment More Than My Own Sometimes

"My daughter is kind of, my financial adviser. I count on her for a lot of things, for a lot of decisions. I respect her judgment more than my own sometimes. It would be a big loss to me, not to have that. I wouldn't trust anybody else, but I do trust her."

Leonard, seventy-three year old ex- school music teacher, father of a forty-six year old son and a thirty-three year old daughter (divorced later in life but has stayed close to his daughter)

Her Illness Has Brought Us Closer – At My Age I Love Being Needed

At My Age It's Good To Have Somebody To Take Care Of

"I love being needed, even though [it's because] my daughter has Multiple Sclerosis. [Her having this illness] has brought us closer.

I don't think she's ever [needed me before]. I feel that she's more affectionate, maybe even more dependent than she's ever been. But still, very much more independent than I would have expected.

> When a daughter becomes ill, a profound instinct is sparked in many dads.
>
> Somehow, being needed by your child creates a sense of deep purpose.
>
> What could be more important than being there in her moment of greatest need?

[She was diagnosed with it] just about six months ago. [The initial signs were a] numbness in her extremities and a feeling of being cold.

I think the biggest fear is, you just don't know what's going to happen. Is it going to happen quickly? Is it going to happen slowly? It's a big question, nobody knows.

Worst case scenario, she would be totally dependent on other people to take care of her. Best case scenario, maybe they can arrest it the way it is and keep it that way. Or maybe even clear it up, but I doubt that.

I think we were close before, but this made us definitely closer.

Of course I'm worried about it. But I'm at a stage of life where I need to be needed. So in a way, it's good for me to have somebody to take care of. I would be very happy to be in that situation now, anyway that she needs it.

For example, with the kind of work she does, she needs a studio. She's renting one, but the pressure is on her to make enough money to pay to make it feasible. So I am going to put an addition on my house and make it into a studio for her, so she doesn't have to pay for it.

I also do a lot of taking care of the grandkids. She calls on me a lot for that. [She has] two daughters, about twelve and nine."

Leonard, seventy-three year old father of a forty-six year old son and a thirty-three year old daughter (divorced later in life but has stayed close to his daughter)

I Love Being A Grandfather

Being A Grandfather—I Can See My Contribution Ripples Forward Into The Future

"[If I'd never had my daughter], first of all I wouldn't have a magnificent grandson.

And I don't think my heart would be as open. I don't know why I said that but that's what comes up. Yeah.

I've really loved being a dad to my kids and to my stepkids, and I love being a grandfather to my grandchildren. I know I've made a contribution to their lives and into their children's lives. That will make a difference on some [level for generations to come] that I won't even know. It's the ripples and the bond [with the future]."

George, seventy-five year old father of fifty-two year old daughter and two sons; also later became stepfather of another daughter (when she was a teenager) and a stepson

Being A Grandfather Is Easier Than Being a Father—I Know More What To Expect

"I love [being a grandfather]. It's much easier than being a father.

My daughter has two daughters, about twelve and nine, and I'm closer to my granddaughters than I was to my daughter.

Here's why.

I do a lot of taking care of the grandkids. She calls on me a lot for that.

[But also], in some ways I think I'm more mature. I have more time and more background. I know more what to expect."

Leonard, seventy-three year old ex- school music teacher, father of a forty-six year old son and a thirty-three year old daughter (divorced later in life but has stayed close to his daughter)

In The End—Nothing Is More Important Than Family

You Can't Replace Family—Once They're Gone They're Gone

"In closing I will just give you one piece of advice. There's nothing, nothing more important than family—as you will find out when you get older.

Blood! As you get older you gotta get closer because you can't replace family. Once they're gone, they're gone.

There's a far distance to travel, I understand all that. But there's telephones, there's emails, there's shmee-mails, there's letters.

You should be close. Closer!

You're all busy trying to make a living. I don't say you should sit on the phone every day. But you should be in touch. There's nothing more important than family."

Walter, eighty-one year old retired businessman, father of a fifty-six year old daughter and three sons

Some Surprises from this Chapter

Dad with a Daughter Over Age Forty-Nine

- **Her Biggest Fan:** It was not surprising that many dads defined themselves as, *"my daughter's biggest fan,"* although most had never actually said that to her. Even among the least connected dads there was generally a sense of pride for their daughters.

- **A Closer Relationship:** Many dads in their seventies and eighties commented on how the relationship with their daughter was closer now than in previous years. Some surmised it was her desire to connect with him before he died, while others felt their age had caused them both to mellow and be more approachable.

- **She Being His Caretaker:** Not surprisingly, most dads who needed to be cared for or administered to by a daughter, generally felt emasculated or humiliated at having to be dependent. Virtually all these dads said they felt like a burden and wished they could be more independent. Many believed the relationship with their daughter suffered from this dependence.

- **Him Being Her Caretaker:** When the tables were turned and a father could take care of his daughter, especially if she became ill, this seemed to bring forth a nurturing instinct in many dads.

- **Father and Grandfather:** A surprising number of dads described the joy they felt at being a grandfather as easier than being a parent because the rules for how to behave were now clearer.

Final Thoughts
On Being a Father to a Daughter

How Has My Daughter Affected Me...

She's Helped Me Move Past My Own Childhood In Some Way

"My daughter makes me feel good to be a man. She makes me feel good to be a dad, makes me proud to be her father. It feels good to be around her. That's how she affects me now.

It's so different than how I grew up. It's just been beautiful to see somebody that's been able to step into their own power. She's stepping into her own light. That's helped me move past my own pain from my childhood in some way."

Mark, forty-four year old Navy pilot, father of a fifteen year old daughter and an eleven year old son (divorced when his daughter was seven but stayed involved as a dad)

My Daughter Has Shown Me The Tender Side Of Myself

"How has {my daughter} Iman affected me?

She has made me laugh. She has made me cry. She's affected all of my emotions. She's probably pulled on every emotional heart string. But {in doing that} she showed me the tender softer side of myself.

She's really introduced me to the arts in terms of ballet. I learned a lot about ballet through Iman.

But I guess ultimately what I learned from Iman is just a sense of—just about the love between a father and a daughter. We just have a great relationship right now. She just makes me laugh {and} she makes me very proud, so I keep that.

This is a hard question for me...

What have I learned?

I just learned to be caring love unconditionally. Yeah, that's where I am."

Darryl, forty-seven year old business executive, father of a seventeen year old son and a fourteen year old daughter

I'm Lucky—Some Dads Don't Have Any Relationship With Their Daughter

Being Estranged From My Daughter Would Break My Heart

"You know, I really should count my blessings, because I have so many friends who are estranged from their children for one reason or another.

That would break my heart. I'm sure it does theirs."

Leonard, seventy-three year old father of a forty-six year old son and a thirty-three year old daughter (divorced later in life but has stayed close to his daughter)

For one of the last interviews a daughter came forward and asked if we would interview her father, a therapist and television personality. She had been estranged from him for almost a decade, but they had recently reconnected. She didn't know what we would ask, but felt our interview would somehow be important. After the interview her dad let her listen to the recording.

"Have you any idea what you've done," she told us, almost accusatory.

Fearing we had done something terrible, we meekly asked, "What did we do?"

"You got my dad to finally talk about the elephant in the room. Since we have reconnected, the one thing we would never talk about was the nine years when he had disappeared from my life. You got my dad to talk about that one thing neither of us would venture to talk about. What you have given us is an incredible gift."

We share this excerpt below from her dad's interview, in the hope that fathers and daughters like us who may not have had the greatest connection, will realize it's never too late.

I Discovered It's Not Too Late To Reconnect With My Daughter

I Disappeared From Her Life For Nine Years—I Can't Get That Time Back

"I never pictured myself as a father. I was always very careful.

[But] once that happened, [once my wife became pregnant] I was completely involved in all the classes, in the delivery room, even taking care of [my daughter]. I took my role and I enjoyed it.

Even during [my daughter's] childhood [and after the divorce] I was completely involved during the times my daughter spent with me. I was devoted one-hundred percent with her, singing with her and playing with her and playing music—very involved with everything, [even with] all her activities in school."

> The greatest gift was hearing from dads who had reconnected with their daughters, sometimes after decades of estrangement.
>
> Not every dad and daughter could reconcile their issues.
>
> But hearing from a few who have, helps us all realize that no matter how broken a relationship is, there may still be hope.

— Then, When She Was Fifteen I Disappeared For Nine Years —

"I [made] a very bad decision. Those were the times my daughter needed me most, and I was not there for her.

[But my new wife didn't want me to have any connection with my previous family], so I decided to separate from my daughter.

[It's funny how a decision like that stays with you. Years later, when] I knew she had moved to New York, every time I was walking in the streets of Manhattan and down in the subway, I would [look around on the odd chance that I might] see her.

In 2006 after nine years, I [finally] talked to her by phone and then I met her in the hotel that I used to stay in.

The night that I found her—that I had the chance to hug her and to talk to her again—that really is something I will never forget in my life.

I'm trying to forgive [myself] for that decision that I took. But I was not worthy in a certain way because I put aside my daughter for someone that, in the end, abandoned me. They showed me it was all about money.

The most [incredible] thing is that my daughter Karla has forgiven me. After all she suffered with that separation, the greatness of Karla is her forgiveness.

To put aside your daughter and not take care of her, not even a call for Christmas, for her birthday, to not be there when she graduates from college, to not to be there at her wedding...

[That Karla is] able to forgive her father—and not only that, [but] now to build a stronger relationship than it was before, that is the greatness of Karla. That is what makes me feel humble in front of her.

Now I feel that I have the chance to really enjoy this relationship in the full sense.

[We have] the most interesting, profound and funny conversations. And we play a lot, we joke a lot, we laugh and laugh and laugh during the night.

And her husband is very funny.

You know, my mother was very funny and my dad was very funny. My mother—she was seventy years old and she used to wear costumes for Halloween and scare all the old ladies in the neighborhood. She was very funny.

So we are kind of a funny family. We don't take ourselves too seriously.

This is very easy for me [because it means] I don't feel that I have to [play] a specific [part] as a father. [I can just be myself]."

– There's No Guide Book On How To Be A Good Father –

"You know, [this parenting thing], this is on-the-job training that you do. Because every human being is an individual, it's a [unique] process [for each of us].

So who has this book of fatherhood? Who can tell [you how to be a good father]?

In my thirty-two years as a therapist, I have not found one single human being. I have a lot of colleagues that are specialists in child psychology, and they cannot teach it, because every human being is [involved in a unique] process. It's a point of view [and it's different for each] person.

I can tell [another father about] my experience. But probably he will have a completely different daughter than Karla. So he will have to deal with her personality and her biological traits—and the mental processes that she has and the emotional process that she has.

[I've discovered with my daughter that] the only thing is to be honest. Whenever you don't have answers, tell her you don't have an answer. Whenever you don't have a tool, confess you don't have a tool. Be honest. Be a friend. Be there when she needs you.

[As a therapist] every time someone sits in front of me in consultation, I cannot [always] apply the rules. That's the reason why sometimes it's [necessary] to have a sense rather than a technique, because you are dealing with [a unique human] process, not dealing with structures."

– If She Had Never Been Part Of My Life, What Would Be Different –

"Everything. Everything. Everything would be different.

She has been a landmark in my life. Even though we had the time of separation, she always has been there [in my mind].

I remember the moment my father and my mother died. They died two years apart. I felt there was a point of reference that I lost.

[In the same way] Karla has always been a point of reference for me. Karla is there, and I feel it. Even [when] we don't talk, I feel it. There's a connection inside that I can make reference [to] psychologically or spiritually or energetically.

[My relationship with her] is one of the most outstanding things in my life. Now I'm back to knowing her and trying to fill all the gaps that happened during those nine years that we were basically separated."

Jose, fifty-four year old therapist and television personality, father of a twenty-eight year old daughter (divorced, and then recently reconnected with his daughter after a nine-year absence—he is humbled that she has forgiven him for abandoning her)

Some Surprises

Final Thoughts

- **Impact of a Daughter on her Dad:** Whether the relationship with his daughter was close or not, it was fascinating that virtually all the dads used the word "profound" to describe the impact of a daughter on him.

  For many, this was the first and only platonic relationship with a female, where he was more interested in mentoring, comforting and protecting than in dating. For most, his daughter had helped him connect to his feelings in a way no one else could. She drew him closer *("I love you daddy,")* then pushed him away. Yet, through thick and thin, she would *always* be his daughter.

  The relationship with a daughter was so impactful, it even helped some dads move past emotional pain that had plagued them since childhood.

- **Reconnecting Later in Life:** From the stories of these dads, an optimism emerged that even a strained or alienated relationship between a father and his daughter could sometimes be restored, even after decades.

- **Not Taking it For Granted:** Perhaps the most significant observation from a few dads, was a feeling of how lucky they were to have a close relationship with their daughter when so many dads did not.

The relationship with his daughter qualifies as the most "permanent" relationship in the life of most dads.

As one dad so aptly put it, *"It's impossible to explain the importance of a daughter to someone who does not have one. A wife could be divorced, you could break up with a girlfriend, but a child is forever."*

"My daughter will be my daughter… until death do us part."

Break Through the Invisible Barrier
between Your Father and You

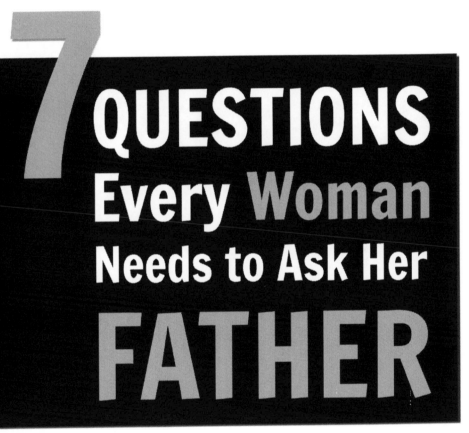

These seven questions are based on the extensive personal interviews we did with 101 fathers of daughters, combined with almost eighteen years of research into human behavior, and why people do what they do.

As featured on:

THE 7 QUESTIONS EVERY WOMAN NEEDS TO ASK HER FATHER

To help you understand your father's heart a little better, and to plant the seeds for a better relationship, here are seven questions every women needs to ask her father.

These questions were developed because, when it comes to expressing their true feelings, many men (and fathers) will not start the process without a little help.

Sometimes one of these questions will touch on such a sensitive emotion that it needs setup, to make it easier for your father to answer. For this reason you will notice the primary question sometimes includes a few setup questions.

QUESTION #1

HOW HAS YOUR FATHER BEEN "AFFECTED" BY YOU?

Ask: If I were never born, what would be different in your life?

Note: Some dads will half-joke that, if you were never born they would have more money. There certainly can be a degree of truth to this, and many dads like to joke as a way of avoiding, particularly when asked a sensitive question.

If he says: "I'd have more money..."

Ask him... Besides having more money, if I had never been born, what would be different in your life?

QUESTION #2

DOES YOUR FATHER UNDERSTAND HOW HE HAS AFFECTED YOU?

Explain: Did you know that, because you were the first man in my life, your words, actions and support of me have affected my confidence and ability to be happy and successful in life?

Then Ask: How do you feel your words and actions have affected me?

What if anything, would you want to be different?

QUESTION #3

HOW DOES YOUR FATHER RATE HIMSELF AS A FATHER?

Ask: What makes a great dad and what makes a terrible dad?

On a scale of 1-10, 10 being best, how do you feel you'd rate yourself as a dad? Why?

QUESTION #4

HOW DOES YOUR FATHER COMMUNICATE WITH YOU (and with women)?

Explain: Men can be really great problem solvers, but are often not that great at just listening, without trying to solve a daughter's every problem.

However, daughters often want to share information without getting her dad to try and solve every problem she has.

Then Ask: Would you be willing sometimes to just listen to my issues without trying to solve my problems?

How could I let you know about those times when I just want you to listen, and maybe to support me (and/or hug me) without trying to solve something?

QUESTION #5

HOW DOES YOUR FATHER EXPRESS HIS LOVE?

Ask: A dog knows you love him because you walk him, you hug him, and you give him treats. How do I know you love me?

(He may respond, I walk you, hug you and give you treats...)

Then ask: What are some of the ways you show me how you really feel about me?

QUESTION #6

WHAT OBSTACLES PREVENT THE TWO OF YOU FROM HAVING A BETTER RELATIONSHIP?

Ask: What are some of the things in your life (or mine) that prevent our relationship from being even better? (job, divorce, new wife/girlfriend, distance).

Is there anything we could do to make our relationship even better? What?

QUESTION #7

UNSPOKEN WORDS... WHAT HAS YOUR FATHER ALWAYS WANTED TO TELL YOU?

Ask: If this were your last day on earth and you could say anything, what would you want to tell me that you haven't already (about you or about our relationship)?

##############################

Try these and watch what happens.

A noted celebrity photographer tried these questions with her dad and something amazing happened.

The father who had been emotionally distant all her life, suddenly opened up about his deep love for her and his overwhelming pride for what she had achieved in her life.

A few months later, he learned that he had terminal cancer, which overtook him quickly. In his waning days, she got to enjoy incredible chats with the father that she felt she barely knew.

The message here is clear. Don't wait until it's too late. If you are willing, try these questions on your dad... and let's see what happens.

Break Through the Invisible Barrier
between Your Daughter and You

3 Simple RULES to Being a Great Dad to a DAUGHTER

GIRLS ARE ALIENS

For dads, raising a daughter is different than raising a son. Ken, a 9/11 New York City fireman with a six year old daughter, explained it best:

> "I grew up in a house with two boys, so to me, girls were aliens."

This amazing dad was among more than a hundred who came forward and agreed to be interviewed for The Father-Daughter Project™.

From these interviews and over a decade of behavioral research, and from our own personal experiences as fathers of daughters, these three simple rules have emerged.

Short and sweet, here are the rules that will help enrich and strengthen the amazing relationship that can only exist between a dad and his daughter, at any age.

Three Simple Rules

➡ Give more **support**, less **advice**.

➡ Do things **together**, just the two of you.

➡ Be truly **present** when you are with your daughter.

Rule #1

➡ As a Dad, are you giving too much **advice** and not enough **support**?

(Guess what...
there is a difference)

This is something many dads do not understand. When your daughter discusses something that's important to her, many Dads instinctively respond by giving "advice". It's something we dads generally do really well.

But to many girls, when we give them advice, it is almost like telling them they are not smart enough to figure things out for themselves.

The message is subtle, but many daughters have told us that deep down they feel this is the underlying message they are getting, when daddy continually gives them advice.

Of course, for many dads, giving advice is our way of showing our love. "We care about you and want to make sure you don't make mistakes."

But women (and definitely daughters) often just want their dad to be there for her; to listen, comfort and support her (and hug her).

For many dads, this can be extremely difficult—just listening without providing advice or feedback. Yet this can be essential to building a strong relationship with your daughter.

Of course, some women love the attention, of daddy (and men) coming to their rescue whenever they have a problem, and even if they don't.

But in general, a daughter needs to know that every time she comes to you with an issue, you won't be automatically rescuing her.

Instead, she wants to be reminded how amazing, smart and competent she is.

In this way, as her dad, you will be boosting her confidence rather than inadvertently tearing it down.

Quick Tip

So here's a simple way to be sure you are doing the right thing with your daughter.

If your daughter tells you something and you want to respond, before giving advice, ask her, "How can daddy help? Do you want my advice or do you want me to just listen and be here for you?"

In this way, you are being strong for her, but allowing your daughter to define what she really needs, and what is important for her.

So here's the big question.

Could you as her father, just listen and be there for her, without giving advice? The strength of your relationship may depend on it.

This is an essential element in developing emotionally healthy daughters—by giving them the ability to "ask" for what they really want when confronted with an important situation.

This simple procedure alone could strengthen in immeasurable ways your relationship with your daughter, boost her self confidence, and make her comfortable coming to you (and others) whenever something important comes up for her.

Rule #2

➡ As her dad, do you
spend time doing
things together,
just the two of you?

It's amazing what a daughter re-members. We chatted with hun-dreds of daughters who recalled a time with their dad, doing something inspiring, uplifting or just fun – that may have happened twenty or even thirty years earlier. These are the mo-ments that become lifelong memories.

Yet, many dads could not recall a time when they did something alone, just with their daughter.

Sure they did the family outings, trips to the zoo and amusement parks, and sporting events. But to recall a time when dad and daughter did something, just the two of them... few dads have this memory.

Some dads solved this by scheduling time,

perhaps once a week or month, where every child got one day or one afternoon alone with dad.

No cell phone. No work. Just something a dad and his daughter could do together.

The best activities include opportunities where dad and daughter could also chat about what's happening in each other's life, rather than sitting in a venue so noisy that you could barely hear yourself think.

It doesn't need to be complicated.

Play a board game, a card game or a word game with just the two of you. Paint a doll house together. Go to a museum together. Create a family scrap book. Or just go for a walk in the park, or for a quiet dinner.

Try it. You'll be amazed at what a simple way this can be to strengthen your relationship.

These are the moments that build lasting memories and bonds between a dad and his daughter.

Don't Wait Until It's Too Late

Sadly, many dads and daughters delay doing anything together, perhaps until there is a divorce.

For others, they never spend time together, chatting about life, having a shared experience — just the two of you.

Our suggestion is, don't wait until it's too late. Set it up now, today, this week.

To jog your mind, here are a few ideas for activities a dad and daughter could do together.

OUTDOOR / INDOOR RECREATION

- Go on a nature walk
- Play board games and word games
- Paint and decorate a doll house
- Visit local and regional parks
- Create a family scrap book or
- genealogy project together
- Play badminton, Frisbee, foosball, tennis, house putting (golf)
- Play or learn golf together
- Go fishing together
- Go go-carting
- Play laser tag
- Learn and go scuba diving together
- Go boating or kayaking
- Learn and experience sky diving, riding the rapids, sports car racing
- Go mountain climbing
- Rough it out in the wilderness to-gether
- Go camping

ARTS AND CULTURE

- Visit an arboretum or museum
- Learn to dance
- Learn a musical instrument together
- Visit local exhibits and displays (check tourist bureaus, arts centers, etc for ideas)
- Visit the theater
- Take stand-up comedy, improv or acting classes together
- Take art, theater or film appreciation classes together

DISCOVERY

- Explore yard sales
- Go shopping, especially to far away or unusual locations
- Visit tourist spots (using a tourist map)
- Go on a car trip (day trips can be great)

DINING

- Explore new restaurants
- Learn cooking, and prepare meals together

ATTRACTIONS

- Visit tourist attractions (get a tourist map, even of your own home town)

- Go to a theme park, zoo, aquarium
- Visit regional exhibits
- Go to a comedy club

EVENTS AND EXPERIENCES

- Learn something together (nature exploring, animal husbandry)
- Go to a sports event – baseball, football, basketball, hockey, boxing, soccer
- Go to the track – car racing, horse or dog racing
- Do volunteer work together (man-ning soup kitchens, Habitat for the Humanities, Feed the Children, visit-ing elderly in hospitals, Make-A-Wish Foundation)

Remember: Don't wait until it's too late.
Set a time now, today, this week.

Rule #3

➡ Are you truly **present** when you are with your daughter?

Perhaps the most important rule we've heard from both dads and daughters is this. If you want an enriching relationship that will withstand the complexities of time, you must "be present" when the two of you are together.

This means, for a single day or afternoon, or just a few minutes that you're with your daughter, don't be on your cell phone. Don't be talking to your buddies. Don't be thinking of work or of something else.

When your daughter asks you something, don't let your mind wander. Instead, truly listen to her. Be an "active listener," engaging with her, and getting her to elaborate, so you truly understand what's going on in her life.

Consider the time with your daughter as therapy for both of you.

This may seem simplistic, but it's not.

Too many dads spend time with their daughters, but their minds are not engaged, or they're distracted. This robs the both of you of the connection that will endure.

Sure you're spending time with her, but are you learning what's happening in her life? Is she learning more about her daddy, or are you just going through the motions?

When done right, the relationship with your daughter will grow in ways that will surprise you, while solidifying what can become one of your closest lifelong connections.

But there's another reason to have this dedicated time together.

It Makes You Smarter and Healthier... Think of it as Therapy

People who learn to take time-off like this, putting their daily issues out of their mind for short periods, tend to be healthier, and in many cases, even smarter.

Archimedes, one of the greatest scientists in human history, was in his bathtub when he discovered the "eureka" moment that changed his life. Isaac Newton was goofing off in an orchard watching apples fall from trees when he got the "eureka" moment that changed his life, and changed our world.

Archimedes and Newton could just as easily have been goofing off, spending time with their daughters when the "eureka" moment struck each of them.

If the "eureka" moment happened when they were with their daughters, the added benefit would have been a greater connection with her.

So take some time right now, put down this

book, and hug your daughter. Both your lives may become infinitely enriched for it.

BEING THERE...
AND YET, NOT BEING THERE

We saw a young dad shopping with his four year old daughter. She was so excited to be with her daddy, but he was busy cackling in idle chatter on his cell phone.

For this dad, he will never be able to reclaim that time with his daughter. One day he will wake up and realize, her life has passed him by with few, if any, memorable moments.

But your life can be better than this!

SO, HERE'S WHAT IT TAKES TO HAVE A GREAT RELATIONSHIP WITH YOUR DAUGHTER

Turn off your phone (don't just put it on vibrate) and spend time with her.

Really be "present" when you're with her.

Listen without giving advice.

And tell her how amazing she is, and how important she is in your life.

Sure there will be moments when you are overcome with emotion, where you may get angry or frustrated with your daughter.

But those moments will pass, and you'll be left with a lasting and profound connection to this person you helped raise.

This person you are connected with... til death do you part.

Share Your Own Father-Daughter Story

If you are a father...
If you are a daughter...
Tell us your story.

At The Father Daughter Project we are devoted to helping improve the relationship between fathers and daughters. In part we do this by enabling and encouraging dads and daughters to talk to each other, and to share their story with others, of what it's like to be a dad or a daughter. You never know how your own story may touch a chord with another dad or daughter.

Share your story. Tell us what it's like to be a father and a daughter. We'd love to hear from you.

Come to our website at www.TheFatherDaughterProject.com.

Also, if you have ideas about how we can all help improve the relationships between fathers and daughters, let us know your ideas or come join The Father-Daughter Project at www.TheFatherDaughterProject.com.

ABOUT THE EDITORS

This work is the result of a collaboration between many caring and devoted people who have been directly and indirectly involved with The Father Daughter Project™. Below is some information about Jim Bond, the principal editor and steward of this work.

James I. Bond, Founder,
The Father-Daughter Project

Jim is founder and president of The Father Daughter Project™, a collaboration of individuals and organizations that have come together to help improve the relationships between fathers and daughters worldwide. We believe that in some small way this great work can help make the world more caring and compassionate, and we are seeking the help and assistance of individuals and organizations worldwide.

Jim is a behavioral management specialist. For more than twelve years he led Leadership Management Associates of California, Inc., as president. Some of the companies that sought his expertise included Amgen, The Muscular Dystrophy Association, Litton Industries, Gannett Media, Tenet Healthcare, Cigna Employee Benefits Companies and Kal Kan Pet Foods.

He has also been involved in regional leadership for The Mankind Project, a non-profit men's training and personal development organization.

Most significantly, Jim is the father of four children. a son age thirty-five and three daughters age twenty-five through thirty-three (he is a father-in-training – he hasn't quite gotten it right yet, but he is trying).

Jim and his wife of 38 years, Pam, reside in Thousand Oaks, California.

Printed in Great Britain
by Amazon